A YUPIAQ WORLDVIEW

A YUPIAQ WORLDVIEW

A Pathway to Ecology and Spirit

A. Oscar Kawagley

WAVELAND

PRESS, INC.

Prospect Heights, Illinois

For information about this book, write or call:
    Waveland Press, Inc.
    P.O. Box 400
    Prospect Heights, Illinois 60070
    (847) 634-0081

Contents

Acknowledgments

One does not do research nor write the results in isolation, especially when dealing with people. I have many people to be thankful to: my late Grandmother Matilda (Kinavin) Oscar, as well as my family and community who taught me the philosophy and ways of the Yupiaq people. Their roles, stories, and teachings have given me strength as I struggled to live in two worlds.

In the academic world of the University of British Columbia, I have my thesis committee, Drs. Vincent D'Oyley (chairman), Ray Barnhardt, and Verna Kirkness to thank. They gave of their time to inspire, encourage, and goad when my resolve in completing studies and planning the research flagged. Sometimes my inner sense was: "At your age, why should you be punishing yourself?" They kept me going. Upon Dr. D'Oyley's retirement, Dr. Jean Barman kindly consented to be the co-chair of my committee. I have been blessed with these people who, having worked with people of different worldviews, are thus familiar with my situation and have made it easier for a Yupiaq man trying to come at things from a different perspective. Dr. Barman applied some timely incentive for me to get off my blessed assurance and get with it. One needs that at times.

The Tribal Council of the Yupiit Nation and the Yupiit School District Board of Education were kind enough to allow me to work in the village of Akiak. They gave me the freedom to observe, review curricula, visit classrooms, and interview teachers and villagers. Otherwise, I would not have been able to accomplish what I set out to do.

The Yupiaq villagers made me welcome, and it was my own sense of respect for the people that perhaps kept the association from becoming closer than it could have been. They inspired, gave ideas, gave criticisms of my sometimes errant viewpoints, and informally shared many intellectual concepts with me. Their values and traditions still persist in spite of barrages from within and without. Thank you, Akiak, home of my father's ancestors!

Jan Steinbright has given invaluable help as the manuscript was being prepared for publication. She made suggestions as to the kind of pictures needed to complement the text; reminded me of additions and changes to make. She was patient and persistent.

Finally, one person stands out who has been mentor, friend, adviser, editor, and constant reminder of the things I have to do— Dr. Ray Barnhardt. Without his help, I would not have gotten this book off the ground. Ray understands and realizes what I am attempting to do. He, and people like him from the Western society, make change for the better possible in pursuit of integration into one world. *Quyana tamarpetci.* Thank you to all of you.

Introduction

The incursion of Western society has brought about many cultural and psychological disruptions to the flow of life in traditional societies. Indigenous peoples have become subservient to the Western system and are confronted with new social structures that they do not always find compatible with their needs. The effects of this assimilative process often include altered child-rearing practices and has brought about shifts from nomadic to sedentary lifestyles, changes in dietary orientation from natural to processed foods (oftentimes with less nutritional value), alterations in design and efficiency of housing, and dependence on numerous government institutions that control what people do. The traditional ways of knowing with the attendant life skills and self-regulating processes on which indigenous people have relied for many generations are usually left along the trail in the name of "progress" (Bodley 1982).

The Western educational system has made an attempt to instill a mechanistic and linear worldview in indigenous cultural contexts previously guided by a typically cyclic worldview. The "modern" view tends to be oriented toward the manipulation of the world's resources—including the people—to make political, social, and economic "progress," with the presumed end result being an advanced quality of life (Berger 1976). This view is reinforced by an underlying notion of "manifest destiny," whereby the Western way of life is considered superior to those of traditional societies (Bodley 1982). Notions such as manifest destiny reflect the historical intent of Western society in its approach to indigenous peoples wherever they were encountered, and the residue of such notions is still present today in the sociopolitical practices of governing institutions regulating the lives of indigenous people in such places as Alaska, Canada, New Zealand, Australia, and Norway.

Most indigenous peoples' worldviews seek harmony and integration with all life, including the spiritual, natural, and human domains (Burger 1990; Knudtson & Suzuki 1992). These three realms permeate traditional worldviews and all aspects of indigenous peoples' lives. Their constructed technology was mediated by nature. Their traditional education processes were carefully constructed around mythology, history, the observation of natural processes and animals' and plants' styles of survival and obtaining food, and use of natural materials to make their tools and implements, all of which was made understandable through thoughtful stories and illustrative examples. This view of the world and approach to education has been brought into jeopardy with the onslaught of Western social systems and institutionalized forms of cultural transmission.

The indigenous peoples of the world have experienced varying degrees of disruption or loss with regard to their traditional lifestyles and worldviews. This disruption has contributed to the many psychosocial maladies that are extant in indigenous societies today. The Western worldview with its aggressive educational practices and technoscience orientation has placed indigenous cultures in "harm's way" (Bodley 1982). These cultures, having been characterized as primitive and backward and therefore wanting, are subjected to an endless stream of assimilative processes to bring their practitioners into mainstream society. The indigenous peoples are forced to live in a constructed and psychic world not of their own making or choosing. Little is left in their lives to remind them of their indigenous culture; nor is there recognition of their indigenous consciousness and its application of intelligence, ingenuity, creativity, and inventiveness in the making of their world.

This is not to say that modernity has brought only negative consequences for indigenous peoples, for benefits have been derived as well. Infant mortality is down and childhood diseases greatly diminished. Disastrous fluctuations in food supplies have been reduced, and modes of transportation and means of communication have improved with telephones, radio, and so forth. However, in balance, the benefits to traditional societies are often offset by the many new psychosocial and physical health ailments, problems of costly and inefficient housing, disruptions in parent-child relationships, domestic violence, suicides, alcohol and drug abuse, and other forms of dysfunctional social behavior; with the vast changes has come a general sense of powerlessness and loss of control over individual lives. Consequently, the issue of the long-term consequences of the collision of contrasting worldviews on the survival of indigenous peoples takes on an urgency that can no longer be ignored. Many studies and reports have addressed these concerns, but nearly all have been from a Western perspective. Rarely has the worldview and value structure underlying the way indigenous people look at such issues been examined and an attempt been made to approach the issues from an indigenous perspective.

Since this study is written from the perspective of a Yupiaq researcher working in a traditional Yupiaq setting, the interpretations and generalizations pertaining to attributes of both the Yupiaq and Western worldviews will be presented as seen through Yupiaq eyes. This is not to deny that Yupiaq and Western societies include within them many variant perspectives and that ideas on values, lifestyles, and interrelationships among the human, natural, and spiritual worlds can differ markedly. Nor is it to ignore the fact that within Western society there are many ideas, practices, and artifacts derived from indigenous peoples throughout the world.

When representing the Western worldview from a Yupiaq perspective, it must be understood that the Yupiaq have experienced particular nuances in thinking, ways of doing things, and other idiosyncracies of the Western world through the envoys of the various institutions established to administer to the needs of the Yupiaq people. From the Yupiaq person's perspective, the constellation of these new values, beliefs, and practices introduced through schooling, religion, government, economics, and numerous technological devices represents a worldview quite distinct from that of the Yupiaq. In Yupiaq eyes, Western society often appears as a monolithic entity, despite the fact that it is made up of many diverse institutions and divergent points of view.

This research will attempt to establish an indigenous platform from which to examine some of these issues, utilizing a case study of a Yupiaq Eskimo community in southwestern Alaska to identify

ways in which the values extant in the competing Western and Yupiaq worldviews affect the lives and choices of the people in that community.

In this book the primary purposes of study are as follows:

1. To examine some of the historical consequences of the intersection of a Western and a Yupiaq worldview.

2. To understand how people in the contemporary Yupiaq community of Akiak, Alaska, have adapted their cultural values and principles to accommodate the intersection of Western and Yupiaq worldviews.

3. To document contemporary Yupiaq practices in the traditional activity and setting of a fish camp and explore implications for the development of social, political, economic, and educational institutions suited to the aspirations of Yupiaq communities and indigenous people generally.

4. To construct an epistemological framework and pedagogical orientation in which the Western and Yupiaq traditions of knowledge generation and utilization can be addressed, particularly as they pertain to the learning and use of scientific knowledge in a traditional Yupiaq environment.

I will identify critical elements of the constellation of values and life principles currently operative in a Yupiaq community and explore the extent to which the existing configuration will allow the Yupiaq to reconstruct a world that will empower them with sufficient control over their own lives and give solidarity in their efforts. One dictionary, Random House, defines *value* as "the quality of anything that renders it desirable or useful" and *principle* as "an accepted or professed rule of action or conduct." The Yupiaq terms that are roughly equivalent in meaning are *piciyarat* (qualities for life) and *yungnaqsarat* (rules of life). The first helps to make a life, while the second helps one to make a living. These are the meanings that will be ascribed to the usage of the terms in this study.

A task of this magnitude requires the eventual narrowing of focus to a few of the most critical values and principles that define the intersection between the Western and indigenous worldviews, so

◀ A portion of the village of Akiak showing a dog team, a government-funded house (at right), a storage shed and a fish trap (center).

that the implications can be examined in such social sectors as political, economic, and educational. The identification of certain core values and principles that are essential to the well-being of Yupiaq society is of central concern, and also the determination of how to make these values and principles an indelible part of a newly constructed school curriculum that can serve to revive and reorient the indigenous peoples to a more harmonious and sustainable life in a rapidly changing world. The exploration of contrasting values and principles in this way may open doors for further research and action to begin to implement initiatives that take the best from the two worlds and reconstruct a world to fit the times.

I will first analyze available information on the lifeways, worldview, and ways of knowing of the Yupiaq people as they have evolved over time and then give a detailed description of the ways in which the people in a particular community and region live their life today. Attention will then shift to a Yupiaq perspective on the practice of science and technology, and how that perspective does or does not come into play in the context of education and schooling. Finally, some implications of the study for the application of science and technology and the practice of schooling in a Yupiaq setting are outlined.

Chapter 1

Yupiaq Worldview
The Meeting of Old and New

Basic philosophical questions are raised in the course of observing and questioning people with respect to notions of inquiry, explanation, technology, science, and religion, as they relate to particular lifeways. Accordingly, *worldview* as discussed here will attempt to answer the questions deftly set out by Barry Lopez: "metaphysics, epistemology, ethics, aesthetics and logic—which pose, in order, the following questions. What is real? What can we understand? How should we behave? What is beautiful? What are the patterns we can rely upon?" (1986:202). To his list will be added *ontology*: Why are we? Is there something greater than the human? Lopez goes on to point out, "The risk we take is of finding our final authority in the metaphors rather than in the land. To inquire into the intricacies of a distant landscape, then, provokes thoughts about one's own interior landscape, and the familiar landscapes of memory. The land urges us to come around to an understanding of ourselves" (247).

The concept of worldview is very closely related to the definitions of culture and cognitive map (Berger, Berger, & Kellner 1974:148). A worldview consists of the principles we acquire to make sense of the world around us. Young people learn these principles, including values, traditions, and customs, from myths, legends, stories, family, community, and examples set by community leaders (Deloria 1991a; Hardwick 1991). The worldview, or cognitive map, is a summation of coping devices that have worked in the past and may or may not be as effective in the present (Netting 1986). Once a worldview has been formed, the people are then able to identify themselves as a unique people. Thus, the worldview enables its possessors to make sense of the world around them, make artifacts to fit their world, generate behavior, and interpret their experiences. As with many other indigenous groups, the worldviews of the traditional Alaska Native peoples have worked well for their practitioners for thousands of years.

Alaska Native Worldview

Among Alaska Native peoples exist many languages and dialects, and as many worldviews or variations thereof. Thus, rather than attempt to describe them all, I will deal first with the more prominent shared characteristics of the Alaska Native worldviews and then focus more specifically on the Yupiaq.

Alaska Native peoples have traditionally tried to live in harmony with the world around them. This has required the construction of an intricate subsistence-based worldview, a complex way of life with specific cultural mandates regarding the ways in which the human being is to relate to other human relatives and the natural and spiritual worlds.

This worldview, as demonstrated historically by the Native peoples of Alaska, contained a highly developed social consciousness and sense of responsibility. As indicated by the writings of outside researchers and observers, Native peoples' myths, rituals, and ceremonies were consistent with their relationship to one another and to their environment (Fienup-Riordan 1990; Freeman, Milton, & Carbyn 1988; Locust 1988). Ann Fienup-Riordan postulates that wisdom, insight, knowledge and power were considered the prerogative of the elders, who were honored and respected in recognition of their achievements (1990:55). Attitude was thought to be as important as action; therefore one was to be careful in thought and action so as not to injure another's mind or offend the spirits of the animals and surrounding environment. For one to have a powerful mind was to be "aware of or awake to its surroundings" (1990:74).

To help practitioners along this reciprocal path, Native peoples developed many rituals and ceremonies with respect to motherhood and child rearing, care of animals, hunting and trapping practices, and related ceremonies for maintaining balance between the human, natural, and spiritual realms. This intricate sense of harmony with all things has been identified by most observers as central to understanding Alaska Native worldviews (Freeman & Carbyn 1988; Locust 1988; Scollon & Scollon 1979). A hallmark of Alaska Native peoples was their success at adapting to ever-changing environmental conditions "while strengthening their cultural integrity" (Bielawski 1990:5). This was demonstrated in their ability to reconstruct and continuously modify their worldviews, so that "new" Native traditions have evolved even up to the present day (Fienup-Riordan 1990).

Fienup-Riordan has called the Alaska Native and other indigenous peoples the "original ecologists" (1990:32). One reason for this is that their worldviews are dependent upon reciprocity—do unto others as you would have them do unto you. All of life is considered recyclable and therefore requires certain ways of caring in order to maintain the cycle. Native people cannot put themselves above other living things because they were all created by the Raven, and all are considered an essential component of the universe. They were able to sustain their traditional subsistence economy because "they possessed appropriate ecological knowledge and suitable methods/technology to exploit resources, possessed a philosophy and environmental ethic to keep exploitative abilities in check, and established ground rules for relationships between humans and animals" (Freeman & Carbyn 1988:7).

Out of this ecologically based emphasis on reciprocity, harmony, and balance have evolved some common values and principles that are embedded in the worldviews of most Alaska Native people. The following excerpt from Mary Muktoyuk's story, "Inupiaq Rules for Living," (1988:65–69) is an example:

> Back then, my parents would give us lessons on correct behavior, back when I was first becoming aware. My parents spoke with great wisdom of things that we did not know about.
>
> Also, when we were small, from time to time someone would kill a polar bear. The people were very happy when a hunter killed a polar bear, for polar bears were considered extremely dangerous then.
>
> Then after they had slept a certain number of nights, they would give thanks for it by dancing. They would give thanks for the polar bear.

Then they would give some pieces of skin for sewing to those who were growing old, and they gave them food, too, because they were thankful for that polar bear and were celebrating it. They tried to make those who were growing old happy, too. These days, people are no longer like that, because we are no longer in our land, and because those wise people of long ago have died, all of them. They would give freely of food or skins for sewing. In those days, they gave and gave freely. They lived a good life then. These days, they no longer live in a good way, for they are no longer as they used to be.

The elders, in those days, we held in great respect. Whatever they told us, we would listen very carefully, trying not to make mistakes when we listened, because we respected them so highly, because they knew much more than we did while we were still growing up. In these times, though, people seem to have stopped doing things in the old way. It is known that they no longer do things as they used to. And these days all of them have become that way. Even if they are close friends or relatives, they are no longer like members of a family.

In the past we were aware that even people who were not closely related seemed like close relatives. Now what was is no more. You no longer see people like those who lived then. These people of one village all lived as close relatives; that's how they used to be. They probably can never be the same again. If somehow they could return to a village of their own, I wonder if they might go back to the way they lived long ago.

This story incorporates three important ethical and moral teachings of Native people, namely, the importance of sharing, the role of cooperation in the extended family, and giving thanks to the creative force. It was the practice of the Native hunter to show his wealth and success as a provider by sharing what he obtained with his fellow villagers and invited guests. "In those days, they gave and gave freely," knowing that they would be repaid in kind, respected and taken care of by others in their time of need. The food had been given freely by nature, so it was only right to share it. Particular attention was given to elders who did not have offspring for support, to widows with children, and to orphans. The gratitude of these less fortunates was considered powerful "medicine" that led to good fortune in future hunts. The more one gave, the happier one would be, and the more likely one would lead a long and satisfied life.

The extended family was important for survival and keeping a bloodline alive but did not necessarily consist only of the blood relatives. It included as family members those associated through marriage and "naming." When a family member died, whoever was named after the deceased became a member of the family and was accorded the kin term of the deceased. Regardless of the familial relationship, "people of one village lived as close relatives" (Muktoyuk 1988).

The Native people continue to maintain a complex kin relationship, with a term for each person. The Yupiaq term for relatives is associated with the word for viscera, with connotations of deeply interconnected feelings. One must acknowledge and take pride in a relationship, and this feeling comes from within. Among the Athabascans, this sense of caring and respect derives from distant time (Nelson 1983) and is reinforced through many rituals and stories. These stories often include events in which humans become animals or vice versa, implying interrelationships with all living things, so care and respect must be shown all humans and nonhumans alike, to maintain harmony and balance.

Inherent in all aspects of Alaska Native worldviews is respect for the spiritual forces that govern the universe, so that following a successful hunt, "they would give thanks for it by dancing" (Muktoyuk 1988:67). The creative force, as manifested in nature, is more profound and powerful than anything the human being can do, because in it is the very essence of all things. Yet within this profound and powerful force are efficiency, economy, and purpose, the expression of which is dependent on the human being. As with other indigenous people, within the Native worldview is the notion that "a spiritual landscape exists within the physical landscape" (Lopez 1986:273). This spiritual landscape provides a platform through which integration with other life forces is achieved. O. B. Bakar notes that "Careful observation was made of animal behavior and the inner qualities and the genius of a particular animal species with a view of deriving spiritual and moral lessons from that animal species. There is a metaphysical basis for the belief that animals have much to teach man concerning the divine wisdom and about his own inner nature" (Bakar 1991:95).

Alaska Native worldviews are oriented toward the synthesis of information gathered from interaction with the natural and spiritual worlds so as to accommodate and live in harmony with natural principles and exhibit the values of sharing, cooperation, and respect. Native people's reciprocity with the natural and spiritual realms implies a form of cross-species interaction that M. Caduto and J. Bruchac point out is perhaps only now being learned by Western scientists: "The science of ecology, the study of the inter-actions between living things and their environments, circles back to the ancient wisdom found in the rich oral traditions of American Indian stories. Time and again the stories have said that all of the living and non-living parts of the Earth are one and that people are a part of that wholeness. Today, Western ecological science agrees" (1989:5).

Yupiaq Worldview

This description of the Yupiaq worldview is drawn from having lived the life of a Yupiaq and having been tutored by the people who embody it. Much of this has not been written before, but where appropriate, I have supplied references to written descriptions of common roots in other indigenous societies.

Alaska is divided into twelve cultural regions, each inhabited by indigenous people who call these places home. Alaska, called the "land of the midnight sun," extends from the Arctic to the subarctic. The ecological systems change markedly as one goes north. The people of the Arctic and subarctic have adapted to these ecosystems and still maintain a viable, sustainable subsistence economy (Netting 1986). The worldviews of the peoples of these regions recognize that the land is a giver of life. The land has become their life and their metaphysic, to the point that they live by the circadian rhythms of the universe in which they are situated.

Historically, the Yukon–Kuskokwim Delta region "supported the largest Eskimo population in the world. As many as fifteen thousand people may have lived in western Alaska in the early 1800s, divided into at least twelve socially and territorially distinct regional populations" (Fienup-Riordan 1990). In my own travels in the delta villages, I have often talked to elders regarding the size of the villages. The late Carl Flynn of Tununak said that his village was so large that they had to have an upper and lower *gasegik*, or community house. The "upper" and "lower" do not mean a caste arrangement, but pertain to the topography of the land. The population was subsequently reduced because of new diseases brought in by explorers, fur traders, and missionaries (Fortuine 1989; Napoleon 1991).

According to Fienup-Riordan, the delta region was able to support a large Yupiaq population because of the many and varied resources: "Scarcity is not nearly as threatening as the popular representation of Eskimos allows" (1990). Yet, I recall stories told by my grandmother and others of periods of starvation due to unusual conditions, such as extreme cold or heavy snow cover, animal and fish cycles at a low point, or bird or animal migration paths changed by heavy rains causing flooding and silty waters or other natural catastrophes.

According to Yupiaq creation mythology, the Yupiaq people were created and emerged at their present location, which is the Yukon–Kuskokwim Delta. The two rivers flowing into the region have laid down a marshy alluvial plain, the tundra, on which the Yupiaq people have lived for many thousands of years. This tundra home is known to have very harsh winters reaching chill factors of – 80 degrees Fahrenheit. The wind blows almost constantly, making wind-driven snowdrifts and blizzards.

The summers are short but provide a sufficient season to accommodate migratory birds by the hundreds of thousands. These include geese, ducks, cranes, sea birds, sea gulls, Arctic terns, swans, and a variety of song birds. The marshy tundra provides nesting areas for the birds as well as food for the young hatchlings. Mosquitoes and flies abound. Summer temperatures may reach + 80 degrees Fahrenheit. Twelve varieties of bushes grow along lakes and streams. Spruce trees, alder, and other types of trees grow on the banks of the Yukon and Kuskokwim rivers. The delta region is criss-crossed by sloughs and streams, as well as many lakes.

Many of the streams and tributaries of the two rivers are spawning grounds for a variety of fish. These include five species of salmon, sheefish, burbot, Dolly Varden, rainbow trout, blackfish, Northern pike, whitefish, grayling, and stickleback. Along the coastal area are found flounder, tomcod, herring, halibut, seals, walruses, and an occasional beluga whale. The beluga were once numerous in the Kuskokwim Bay.

The animals that the land provides include moose, caribou, beaver, mink, muskrat, land otter, marten, lynx, snowshoe and Arctic hare, wolf, bear, and foxes. These provide food and/or clothing for the Yupiaq people.

The outsiders' perception that the tundra is inhospitable for humans and relatively lacking in natural resources kept the Yupiaq people isolated for many years, after the Russians explored the region and after its later purchase by the United States. The first externally induced developments in the region were the fur industry, commercial fishing, and mining.

Some Yupiaq men become skillful fish cutters.

According to anthropologists, the precontact Yupiaq villages consisted of 50 to 250 people in each, and the population may have reached 15,000 altogether in the delta region (Fienup-Riordan 1990). Consensus was the means of decision making, and the government egalitarian or communitarian. To accommodate this type of governance, the Yupiaq numbers would have to remain relatively small. Today, we have villages ranging from 25 to 1,000 Yupiaq people, and the total Yupiaq population is over 21,000 people.

The original Yupiaq based their philosophy and lifeways on maintaining and sustaining a balance among the human, natural, and spiritual worlds. They made their winter and summer settlements a part of nature, disturbing the environment as little as possible. Their rituals and ceremonies were intended to help maintain this balance and to regain it if messages from nature and the spiritual realm so indicated. Year after year these ceremonies were performed in exactly the same way, with the idea that someone performing or observing would gain intuitive understanding of something that the person had not understood before.

The balance of nature, or ecological perspective, was of utmost importance to the Yupiaq. History and archeological findings of different races in the world seem to indicate a common philosophical or ecological thread among all people, and this apparent linking leads to the concept of interconnectedness of all things of the universe. The Yupiaq people were, and still are, proponents of this worldview, in spite of the weakening of the ecological perspective by modern intrusions.

To understand the Yupiaq worldview it is necessary to understand the multiple meanings of a word that epitomizes Yupiaq philosophy. This word is *ella*, which is a base word that can be modified to change its meaning by adding a suffix or suffixes. Examples are: *Qaill' ella auqa?* 'How's the weather?'; *Qaill' ellan auqa?* 'How are you feeling?'; *Ellam nunii* 'The world's land'; *Ellagpiim yua* 'Spirit of the Universe'; *Ellapak* 'Universe'; *Ella amigligtuq* 'The sky is cloudy.' Variations of this one word can be made to refer to weather, awareness, world, creative force or god, universe, and sky. The key word is awareness, or consciousness. Consciousness is the highest attainment of the human being, and we must keep in mind that it is not attributable to any one race. The human being must possess consciousness to be able to make sense out of values and traditions as juxtaposed with the "objects" of the universe. As a manifestation of their *ella*, the Yupiaq developed a body of values and traditions that would enable them to maintain and sustain their ecological worldview.

To help illustrate the interrelationship among human nature, nature, and supernature (or spirituality) in the Yupiaq worldview, I will utilize a tetrahedral metaphor (see diagram). The tetrahedral structure, a device recognized for its strength by engineers, is often utilized in the Yupiaq fish or hunting camp by erecting a tripod of wooden poles to hold up game and drying meat or fish. The structure of the tetrahedron allows for several important dynamic forces to be examined in relation to one another. If we use the three corners of the base to represent the human being, nature, and spirituality respectively as elements in a common circle of life, we can see the apex as representing the worldview that overarches and unites the base elements of our existence. The lines connecting these "poles" can be seen as the life forces that flow all ways between and among the human, spiritual, and natural worlds and are united through the worldview. The three base poles all provide essential supports to the Yupiaq worldview.

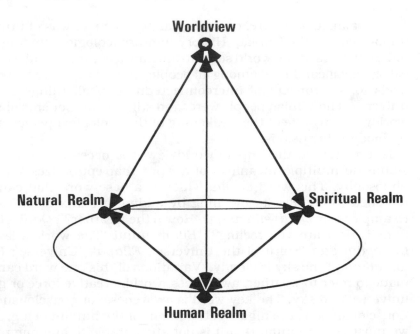

This tetrahedral framework allows for triangulation whereby human beings can locate themselves in relation to the other domains of their existence and check to make sure that the values and traditions are in balance. It illustrates that the Yupiaq worldview is based on an alliance and alignment of all elements and that there must be constant communication between the three constituent realms to maintain this delicate balance. When everything is in alignment, it is an exceptionally strong structure. It does not require earth-shaking change, however, to upset the balance. The Yupiaq would agree with Chief Seattle (1790–1866), who stated that

"This we know: the earth does not belong to man, man belongs to earth. All things are connected like the blood that unites us all. Man did not weave the web of life, he is merely a strand in it. Whatever he does to the web, he does to himself" (qtd. in Vanderwerth 1971).

The tetrahedral universe requires constant communication between the three base realms. This reciprocity of conversations and interrogations is an essential element to the worldview. It allows for ongoing monitoring to make sure that the balance is there. The most important fact shown by this construct is that the human being is a key figure, but not one who stands apart from or above the other elements. The human being is a participant-observer in this universe. We, the human beings, having consciousness and reasoning ability, are the ones who pose questions and devise methodologies for learning about the world around us. Therefore, we are the keys to understanding life and living things and trying to solve the conundrums of nature and our inner worlds. That structure is functional which requires the least amount of thought and manipulation, the least amount of effort and resources, and whose purpose becomes evident with observation and thought. A priori, natural laws are placed in the universe to guide the human beings' thoughts and actions.

What are the conditions in which this worldview works with efficiency, economy and purpose? As young children the traditional Yupiaq people were given specially ground lenses through which to view their world. The resulting cultural map was contained in their language, myths, legends and stories, science and technology, and role models from the community. This oral orientation and learning by observation worked to their advantage. To hear stories being told in the qasegiq (community house) allowed the children and other hearers to savor the words and visualize the events. For the duration of the story, they became a part of the imagery. The modern written word is useful for many things, but it removes the reader from the human interaction element. In the qasegiq, the hearer becomes a part of the story, an essential participant-observer in the events. All participants in the storytelling are expected to behave, not only by the elders, but by all community members. So the child is not only listening quietly but is learning self-discipline and respect for the rights of others. The children learn and the grown-ups are reminded of who and what they are, where they came from, and how they are to interact with others, with natural things and with spirits. This is truly living history.

Our creation myths say that Raven is the creator. Some say that the creative force took the form of the Raven to make the world so that the Yupiaq will never think that they are above the creatures of the earth. How can they be when their creator is a creature of earth? Similarly, modern biology has come to a conclusion that "there exists no objective basis on which to elevate one species over another" (Augros & Stanciu 1987).

The type of governance structure created for this ecological mindset is of utmost importance. Yupiaq thought holds that all creatures, including humans, are born equal. This does not imply that all functions or jobs of the creatures are equal but, rather, that each does its job equally well. All human beings are equal as they have been endowed with consciousness, thus having the ability to develop culturally, intellectually, and morally, each in its own way. Each individual human being in this type of government is afforded the greatest freedom in pursuing the paths available for making a living and living a life. Let us consider two statements. Lester Milbrath (1989:78) says that "being autonomous is being the origin of one's own actions." Michael J. Roads (1987:43) says that the endosomatic sense makers of humanity are "both your freedom of expression and walls of your prison." So it is with the Yupiaq person in seeking knowledge. This quest for knowledge that will open the road to making a living is rigorously sought through the use of the five physical senses, well sprinkled with intuition. From the juggling of values and traditions in the life of the Yupiaq comes the wisdom to make a life.

The Yupiaq person's methodologies include observation, experience, social interaction, and listening to the conversations and interrogations of the natural and spiritual worlds with the mind. The person is always a participant-observer. Roads captures the Yupiaq way succinctly: "To inquire suggests that we seek always to explore rather than exploit—to seek, rather than find—to live life as an open-ended agreement with God, rather than search for a nonexistent conclusion" (1987:132). He goes on to write that "separation and connection, fragmentation and wholeness—all are strands in a single universal thread. While all threads are woven into the human experience as one energy, it is we who separate the strands" (148).

There are a number of values that are important to this worldview. Milbrath (1989) has written that some idea or some practice becomes a value when a feeling has been attached to it. An example of this might be the Yupiaq value of sharing. No one knows when it became a value, but it is likely that it took a very long time to come to mean what it does today. Over the years, Yupiaq people may have found that owning many things was hazardous to their well-being and their nomadic way of life. The pros and cons of owning versus sharing were probably considered, discussed, and practices from other societies observed. On the other hand, maybe because of their spirituality they did not have to go through this process. However it happened, eventually through a lengthy process of observation, experimentation, and reflection, they found that sharing was the best policy for them. Not only were they to share with one another but also with the rest of their world. This was done to recognize and acknowledge the interconnectedness of the universe. They realized the value of sharing when they understood that to have little or nothing is to treasure everything, and it fit very nicely into their ecological mindset. They found that to restrict wants was to always have enough, and they created ways to enjoy to the utmost that which they had.

Cooperation is another valued condition. The Yupiaq worldview is premised on cooperation between the human and natural worlds; therefore it adapts well to the circadian rhythm of the universe. Earlier Yupiaq may have experienced or envisioned circumstances in which irresponsible individualism lead to ambition and avarice, so that the negative effects of ambition for power and avarice for owning things became apparent to them in some way. In the Yupiaq tetrahedral model of a worldview, cooperation seems to be a condition of the universe, for without it balance is difficult to achieve.

In order to work, the Yupiaq worldview required a respect for the wisdom of the elders. A few people in each community would reach very old age. Some grew so old that when they sat on the floor of the qasegiq with their knees bent and elevated, their heads would extend below the knee level. There were others whose teeth had been worn to the gum level. Those who had lost their teeth required food to be chewed by family members for consumption. These people were well cared for, honored and respected for their knowledge and wisdom. This respect was extended to the aged who completed the life cycle by entering the "second childhood," in which they once again were accorded care and nurturing. The attainment of knowledge and respect was based on their reasoning ability and accumulated experience.

One other Yupiaq value that deserves attention is the value of the extended family, not only for survival but to be very aware and appreciative of the blood line. It was so important that special terms and an elaborate system of relationships were devised. These relationships formed people's identity—who they were, where they were from, and what they represented. A person had to have a dynamic sense of self-esteem, self-confidence, and pride without arrogance to survive in a very harsh environment.

Traditionally, men and women had very defined roles. The man was the provider, the one to work with nature in hunting and trapping. It was a solitary effort—solitary in that he did many activities by himself, but in reality was always accompanied by spirits and in close contact with the animals and earth. His role as provider was to learn as much as possible from his father, extended family members, elders and others, so as to be a success.

The woman, on the other hand, had to learn womanly duties from her mother, grandmother, and others. This included child rearing, food preparation, garment making, observing taboos having to do with menses and giving childbirth, and mindfully supporting her husband. The man's success as hunter was just as much her responsibility. They made up a team, complemented one another, and were very much equal in standing. The community members' bondedness to each other was mutual, adding to their wholeness and vitality.

When a child was born, the name of a recently deceased person was anointed to the newborn by pouring a little water into the mouth or sometimes sprinkling onto the head. Thereafter, that was his/her name. The gender was unimportant. The relatives called the baby by that name and the kinship term associated with the person whose name was bestowed on the child. For example, if the deceased person's wife addressed the child, she would address it by name, then follow it with "my husband." Thus, a "new relative" was made whether blood related or not.

The traditional houses in which families lived were constructed of sod in a semi-subterranean fashion. A high, dry location was chosen, a circular hole dug down three to four feet in depth, and then a framework of driftwood was constructed. Sod was cut and carried to the site and placed on the wood frame with the vegetation-covered side next to the wood. Sometimes grass was placed between to serve as a natural vapor barrier. An opening at the top was covered with a seal or walrus gut canopy. This was removed when a fire was made in the firepit for cooking or a fire bath. The house was a circular and domed structure with an enclosed entranceway much like the snow igloos of Northern Canada.

The structure of the Yupiaq sod house has been likened to the woman's reproductive system. The ceiling's name in the Yupiaq language means "the above covering" a term which is now used to mean "heaven." The skylight is likened to the umbilical cord leading to the Ellam Yua, the interior to the womb, and the tunnel-like entrance to the birth canal, or "the way to go out." In the old days, when a person died, he or she was never removed through the entranceway, however, but through the skylight. The body was lifted and passed through the opening to the place of interment. The act was very symbolic of the spirit's journey to the spiritual land. The body was then placed with knees to the chest and arms around the knees bound together at the wrists—a fetal position, perhaps signifying completion of the life cycle and readiness for reincarnation and renewal. The body was then covered with driftwood or rocks, or sometimes with wooden planks, a canoe or kayak overturned with the body inside.

The qasegiq was mainly the domain of men and boys prior to puberty. This is where much of the storytelling, teaching of arts and crafts, tests of skill and strength, and learning of rituals and ceremonies took place. It was the site of reintegration and renewal of spirit and where balancing occurred. When special ceremonies were conducted, participants from other villages were invited. The whole community and visitors from invited communities all participated and enjoyed the generosity of the host village. They renewed acquaintances and made new friendships, acknowledged the unseen greater powers, paid respects to their ancestors, celebrated the animal spirits, and even made a few marriage arrangements. The ceremonies reaffirmed the truths that the people chose to live by.

The social structure of the Yupiaq people was maintained primarily at the extended family level. Perhaps by observing and recounting stories, they came to the conclusion that chaos would result when a certain population balance was exceeded. To work, the Yupiaq worldview and governance required a stable and constant population. To come to this understanding, the early Yupiaq might have observed other socially organized animals, such as wolves, beaver, bees, and ants. In each case, they realized that when the population reached a critical level, the leadership of the group would slough off a certain number to start their own new group or succumb to the elements. An additional factor for the Yupiaq people was the high birth mortality and short life span of most mature people; both helped keep the population constant. Not only did this population balance give stability, but it kept to a minimum the "status tension" (Morris 1969:38) present in larger social systems. The limited number fostered collective tolerance by the Yupiaq people and allowed for communitarianism to work.

This self-governing population level allowed the Yupiaq people to live a satisfactory life, in balance with the carrying capacity of the land and waters. Modern communities, with their technological infrastructure, tend to ignore the confusion and social chaos that can occur when too many people congregate in a large city or village. The profusion of laws needed to regulate the conduct of people then obfuscates who they are and how they are to act.

The Yupiaq teachings of humility and tenderness to all human beings and things promoted tolerance. Hand in hand to this is a sense of humor that teaches the individual not to take oneself too seriously, to laugh with others at oneself, and to use humor to teach another not to repeat an unacceptable act.

For matters of survival, the Yupiaq found that it was necessary to learn much about their immediate landscape. Of course, a few of their people had made exploratory forays into other parts of the world, and sometimes the "explorer" did not have a choice because a storm took him off course or he got caught by ice and had to go wherever it went. The Yupiaq have many stories of this type. It was important to know intimately the land on which they dwelled. As Lopez put it, "one is better off with a precise and local knowledge, and a wariness of borders" (1986:259). Lopez goes on to say that the land makes the myths real and, subsequently, the people as well.

The Yupiaq worldview of harmony with one's surroundings was reinforced by the construction of houses and storage shelters made of natural materials, so as to be one with and of nature. This is reflected in the statement by Desmond Morris, "A genuine village, seen from the air, looks like an organic growth, not a piece of slide-rule geometry, a point which most planners seem studiously to ignore" (1969:197). This value of being with and of nature gave a social identity to the Yupiaq, which is in contrast to the geometric detachment reflected in the design of villages today. To insure balance in their worldview it was necessary to consider earth as a resource for living. Thom Alcoze has stated that "we have to turn to a people, a culture, where you don't have to prove that the earth is alive. It's understood. It is the fundamental basis of Native cultures throughout indigenous global society. The earth, she is our mother" (cited in Greer 1992:18). Therefore, for the Yupiaq, there was no need to separate the things of earth into living versus nonliving or renewable versus nonrenewable. Doing so would essentially bifurcate and breach the concept of interconnectedness.

As the tetrahedron suggests, the Yupiaq infrastructure had to include a dynamic sense of sacredness, and as Richard Nelson has written, wherever the Native person is, that place serves as a kind of cathedral, deserving of respectful behavior (1983). This deep sense of sacredness was compatible with the Yupiaq's nature-mediated technology whereby the hunting implements and tools were themselves made of natural materials and thus were less likely to offend the hunted animal. To ensure that balance was always maintained or regained, the Yupiaq created rituals and ceremonies with songs, dances, and all the needed accoutrements. The paraphernalia included masks, which were often an attempt at reification of a vision, dream, or unusual experience. They always included a story with attendant values. Very often the mask was an experience that a shaman had. Upon the shaman's return he or she would render the experience into a mask, using wood, stone, bone, feathers, and natural paints. If the shaman was not given to carving, then he or she would have a carver carve the mask under careful guidance.

In concert with all of the above was and is the giving of thanks to the Ellam Yua, the Spirit of the Universe. This was and is done through rituals, ceremonies, singing, and dancing, which reinforce the belief that all nature is alive and everything has its own being. These activities allow people to spiritually center themselves, reintegrate their relationship to nature and supernature, renew or gain new friendships, share, joke, and laugh, size up possible husbands or wives for marriageable offspring, and thus ensure harmony and sustainability.

For Native people, teaching and learning was holistic and an integral part of everyday life (Bielawski 1990; Wilson 1969). Culturally appropriate knowledge was gained through activity as well as contemplation and observation, and production of knowledge was also a social activity (Bielawski 1990) "Inuit knowledge is consensual, replicable, generalizable, incorporating, and to some extent experimental and predictive" (Bielawski 1990:15). "Predictions" were made on the coming winter's weather, plentifulness or scarcity of fish for the following summer, the coming summer's berries and where they will be most plentiful, and so on. This was done by observing and reading the sign-makers of nature, and it reflects the power of the thinking Native mind. Predictions were made based on observable phenomena.

In distant time, education was well suited to the people and to their ecological systems (Nelson 1983). Education was a part of life. It was provided effectively and stress free by parents, family, extended family, and the community (Darnell 1979; Hopson 1977). Every member knew that all would have a part in the community and be a contributing member. They took care of the community and the community took care of them. The foremost purpose of traditional education was to insure that the principles or rules for constructing a cognitive map for life were learned well by all people (Spradley 1980). From this they would make tools for making a living. The environment was their school and their cathedral, and reading its natural processes gave meaning to all life. The elders were there to give guidance with natural meanings and spiritual matters.

Yupiaq Ways of Knowing: An Illustration

To help illustrate how the many elements of a Yupiaq worldview are manifested and integrated in the teachings of Yupiaq people, I will include here a story with many lessons, first told to me in Yup'ik by my grandmother, under whose tutelage I was raised.

When the earth's crust was thin, there came into consciousness two sparks of life, a girl and a boy. As they surveyed and explored the remnants of a very large village, they often were puzzled: What had happened to cause the people to vanish? Why were she and her male friend alive? How did they survive? A conundrum only to be possibly answered by the supernature!

The old village was located on a river that emptied into the ocean not too far distant. The village faced south, the river flowed west. The flood plain on which it sat was bordered by mountains to the north. The village had been very large, judging by the number of houses in various stages of decay. Their house was in good repair, the cache full of much food and furs.

Each of these young people had to learn their roles by patiently studying, observing, experimenting with, and discussing how their clothing was made and the use of tools and hunting implements. Visions or dreams would come to them as to what to do and how to do it. In pondering the makeup of the mukluk or the parka for many days, she would tire of it and leave it alone, and then one day the idea would come to her—use the bone needle and make thread for it out of sinew. He learned to launch the *qayaq* and use the paddles for propulsion. Their minds were young and receptive to ideas for working with the things at hand and in their world. Watching the grass bend in the breeze, he pulled on a tree limb and watched it spring back. Curiously, he put a stick on it, repeated the motion and watched it being propelled, and suddenly thought, what about that curved stick with sinew attached, and the sticks with feathers in one end and a pointed rock on the other end? Thus came into being the bow and arrow, followed closely by the bow and drill for starting fires. So they grew and expanded their world always as participants.

They eventually became a couple and had a child. They were rich in food and clothing and independence. The man in his hunting always searched for others like themselves or for any signs whenever he went out. One day he returned from the ocean carrying a piece of wood that had not been cut by an animal but with a tool. Then they knew that there must be others somewhere. One day the husband prepared to go on an extended trip to explore further than he had ever done. He said that he would go out to the ocean and follow the coastline around the bend, which must be a peninsula. He took enough food to last several days.

Several days passed—no husband. A moon passes into fall. Winter is upon them. No husband. Food is still plentiful. Summer comes and passes twice. During the spring of the thrice-arriving summer, food is short. She must now soak skins to remove hairs, and then boil it for food. One spring day, she climbs again to the top of the house facing the ocean. The sun is warming, but she is now skinny and must wear her hood. She cries for her lost husband, her son, and herself. She wipes the tears away and looks around. There is nothing to be seen. She again cries. She distinctly hears a voice saying:

"Pitegcurli has married two ladies on the other side of the mountain, Curlik."

Clearing her eyes, she looked around. The only thing in sight is a little dark bird with a red breast.

"Aye! Aye! Who is talking?"

Silence.

Then the little bird opens its mouth, and repeats its song.

"All right, if this is true, show me the direction of his place."

Fish skin bag used for carrying dry fish, berries and other subsistence foods. (Photo by Jean Carlo. Courtesy of Institute of Alaska Native Arts)

Yupiaq woven grass utility bag used for extra clothing, dry fish, frozen fish and other dry goods. (Photo by James Barker)

Without another word, the bird takes to the air. It follows what might have been a trail through the woods, streaks for a pass, and disappears over it.

"So my husband is not dead! It will take me days with my child just to get to the mountains. My child will get tired. I must find some other means to get me there."

She ponders the problem. The solution slowly emerges in her mind—use an animal! She goes up to the cache and examines the animal skins. As she picks up each, she thinks of the attributes and weaknesses of each. The caribou is fleet of foot and has food in abundance for it; however, it tires easily, would not have sure footing on rocks, and has enemies like the wolf, so she decides against it. She examines many skins and finally comes upon a bearskin.

"Now this is the animal. It has no enemies, no shortage of food, has great strength, and won't tire easily. It has no problems climbing nor descending a mountain. This is my choice."

She takes it down, fills a wooden bowl with water, and soaks the skin. While it is soaking, she prepares what little food she has for the child. She tells him that she will be gone for some time and for him to wait for her. She goes out and finds that the skin is softening. She removes it and hangs it until the water has dripped off. She gets down on her hands and knees and throws the skin over herself. It is too large! The stomach reaches to the ground. She thinks, runs into the house, comes out with her large cutting board, places it on her back and throws the skin over her once more. This time it seems that it will fit. She removes all, goes into the house, and reassures her son that she will be gone only for a while. She then places a walrus skin over the door and weights it down. She is now ready for a transformation.

She goes to the bearskin and quietly begins to talk to it. "I am in need of your help. My husband has been gone for a long time. I am told that he is alive and living on the other side of that mountain. As I have taken good care of you when you gave yourself to my husband, now I am asking for your help."

With that she kneels, places the cutting board upon her back and the skin over her. Lo and behold, the skin closes in on her, attaching itself to her, and they become one. She runs toward the mountain. Before long, she is at the pass looking down at another valley. A river meanders down it. Close to the mouth is a house with smoke coming from the skylight. As she watches, a young lady comes out, wanders to the riverbank, and intently looks seaward. Soon she returns to the house. Soon another lady in a different parka repeats the actions of the other. This must be the place.

She goes down, removes the skin and board, and places them on the ground, telling the skin to be ready when she needs it. She walks to the house, stepping lively so as to be heard by those within. She enters the house. There are two surprised ladies sitting beside the firepit, both with cooking pots over the fire. She quickly scans the room and sees her husband's clothes that she had made for him on the bench.

"*Wagaa!* Where did you come from?" said one of the women.

"I've been looking for others like myself for quite some time. I just happened to see your house and was very glad and curious to see who it was."

"Do you live far?"

"Yes, I do."

"You wouldn't happen to be our husband's wife, would you? He has told us that he has a wife," asked the other suspiciously.

"No, I have always lived by myself."

"You are so good-looking! How did you get those marks on your chin?" asked the first.

"Well, you know at one time I was homely. But one day I was cooking, just as you are doing now. I had a thought, so I quickly dipped my ladle into the boiling broth and drank it quickly. The pain was so much that I became unconscious. When I came to, I went over to the pail and looked in. I had become lovely with these beautiful markings on my chin. Would you like to try?"

"Yes," they both answered.

"Now when I say go, both of you dip into the broth and drink as fast as you can, no matter how much it hurts. Are you ready? Go!"

They soon were stretched out dead. Before this act, they had told her that their husband had a strange request—that when he returned from hunting in the ocean, they were to dance for him. She dragged the bodies down by the river, erected two posts, and hung them on it, the parkas placed over the posts with the top end in the hood.

Old Yupiaq bentwood bowls owned by the author. (Photo by James Barker)

She waited. Soon there was a rhythmical glistening in the distance. As it got closer, she could see it was a qayaq. Soon she recognized her husband. He began to sing, but the women never moved.

"Why is it you don't dance?" he screamed.

He grounded his qayaq, jumped out, ran to one, and grabbed it by the arm. It just swung around. He worriedly walked to the other.

"They are dead!" Disbelief turns to rage. "Who could have done this? I will kill whatever killed them."

The wife slowly stands up from the tall grass. "I killed them because they kept you away and let us suffer all these years."

"You meddle in my life! I will kill you!" He runs to his qayaq and takes out his bow and arrow. He starts toward her. She slowly kneels down and says to the bearskin, "NOW!" He is running toward her hiding place. She rears up. He stops, assesses his situation, and pleads with her not to harm him. She bounds toward him. He runs toward the cache and begins to climb. She just barely reaches his leg, pulls him down, pummels,

Kayak and Man, doll by Rosalie Paniyak of Chevak, Alaska. (Photo by James Barker)

tears, and rips him apart. She goes to the other bodies and does the same. Then she enters the house and rips it apart. Finally, the anger dissipates and disappears, and her rational self returns.

"Oh, my anger, now I am alone. My son! I must return."

She quickly returns to her house. Her son is crying inside. She must hurry, she must remove the skin. Try as she will, she cannot. In her frustration she bellows, runs around the house, and as she nears the entrance, rears on her hind legs and with another bellow hits the side of the house with all her strength. The house collapses. A little bird flies out and hovers around its mother, the bear. To this day, the Yupiaq say that a bear is unpredictable because of the woman, and that there is a certain little bird that is always very close to it because of their past kinship.

Myths are the Alaska Native's tool for teaching. The human values that make me uniquely Yupiaq in cadence with the circadian and life rhythms of the universe are all slowly unfolded as my grandmother and other elders teach me through myths and legends. Just exactly how did my people get to know so much about the world and reality?

As I contemplate this question and reflect back to the stories my grandmother told me, I begin to see that the tools for teaching a culture, a science, a way of knowing have always been with us. I know my people are intelligent and ingenious as reflected in their metaphysics and handicrafts, including the snowgoggles, the qayaq, snowshoes, and specialized use of furs for clothing. How then did this come about?

The story my grandmother told me has all the feelings of a human being: peace and harmony, sadness, hunger, jealousy, anger, remorse, and so forth. The Yupiaq have many stories, this one included, in which a human being changes readily from human to animal form. The animals are considered to wear a special parka characterizing each as the animal it represents. All they need to do is remove the hood by taking hold of it at the chin and pulling upward and backward, and behold, a human head is revealed. In this story, the robin is the communicator of the message to the woman. As she considers which animal parka to use, she already has intimate knowledge of the animals' behavior and needs. This is because, when the earth's crust was thin, the humans and animals were accepting of one another and saw no problem with changing into another form of which they were a member already. After all, they believed in Ellam Yua, the Spirit of the Universe. However, they were created by the Raven, so how could they be better than or superior to other animals, plants, and the earth? Some shamans and lost hunters spent up to a year with animal people. During that time they learned their behaviors, their likes and dislikes, and how they were to be treated when they gave of themselves to the hunter. There was ready communication between humans and animals, displaying a feeling of oneness, a unity of being.

Much has been said of intuition as a way of knowing deriving from the unconscious mind, but in an interconnected world even the unconscious is attuned to the forces of nature. Intuition and knowledge made the woman in this story choose the bear. It was only her extreme and uncontrollable anger that made the parka permanently attach to her body. Therefore, we have the admonition to meekness and moderation, even-temperedness and slowness to anger.

Shamans and certain other individuals with no particular credentials were given to visions and dreams. Shamans were trained to have visions via a pot of water, through an animal's eyes, through a star, and other means. These abilities were referred to as Tangruak or 'pretend to see,' and the visions were often brought to fruition. Dreams often told of the future, especially with respect to an individual's impending death. The shaman could tell by the "picture" or aura of a sick individual whether he or she would be ill for a long time, get well, or die. He could tell why animals were scarce for a particular time. He was an expert in human nature and the spirit world and could project himself out of his body to other places known or unknown. The shaman was a messenger between nature, human beings, and the supernatural, and he commuted easily and readily between them.

The elders and others would talk about conditions of their environment when there was plenty of food—conditions that portended a scarce season. After several seasons, as they reviewed their observations orally, they would serendipitously discover the sense makers of nature telling them what to expect. They would note these and discuss them among themselves—the years of plenty and those of scarcity. Out of this would come natural control of births, elders saying to all, "Now is not the time to bear children." They also needed to know how cold and how long the winter would be. Again, nature would give them indicators, as long as they were willing to observe, learn, and apply knowledge to ensure continuation of the people. There were times of sickness also, but it is said that there would always be a number of people unaffected whose task was to care and provide for others unable to do so.

The Yupiaq people made many serendipitous discoveries: wolverine fur resists frosting; polar bear fur is especially good for absorbing radiant energy; pants and parka of caribou with the fur inside is as good or better than a wetsuit; walrus and seal intestines make excellent rainwear, and so on. They devised a system of architecture and engineering to construct the qayaq for strength, seaworthiness, flexibility, stability, carrying capacity, resiliency, transportability, and streamlining, so as to assure the user that he can trust its performance unequivocally.

Yupiaq knowledge was based on a blending of the pragmatic, inductive, and spiritual realms. The shamans and artists brought to the Yupiaq the by-laws of life, inscribed indelibly into their tools, both intellectual and material. They had the flexibility of thought necessary to use the conscious levels of thinking and to have easy access to the subconscious mind. The shaman had the added dimension of access to the spiritual world to solve the conundrums, or puzzles, presented by nature. His function was to explore and interpret what he saw creatively and positively, with the insights to be taught to his people.

One cannot be aware of others or things around one without consciousness, so for the Yupiaq, its meaning is embedded inextricably into the short but all-inclusive base word *ella*. It epitomizes the Yupiaq worldview of interconnectedness, so that you cannot exclude the consciousness of the human observer. Our mystical knowledge cannot have been gained merely by observation, which is the main basis for rational knowledge. To obtain mystical knowledge, observation must be coupled with the participation of our whole being—mind, body, and soul—with the universe. Culture has much to do with our state of mind, and the stories are a necessary tool for the transmission of appropriate attitudes and values of mind. Culture also gives hope to its members that the attitudes and values, and thus the things that make them uniquely themselves, will never be lost but will continue on, regardless of internal or external changes.

Visualization implies a delicate awareness of things perceived visually, through the mind's eye, including visions of the supernatural. Art may be thought of as a process, an idea, or a symbol to bring to an intelligible level an idea shared by a group of people. The making of masks is an expression of what one has experienced through one of the many levels of thinking. It is bringing into a tangible level the experience one has seen or had in the world beyond. Art is the essence of this. Take for a moment a story of a man's seal-hunting trip as expressed in a Yupiaq dance. It will tell of his preparation, his expending of energy to get there, the behavior of his prey, his pride and joy in being successfully given a catch, and the reciprocation of making the seal welcome and using all of it for clothing and sustenance for the family and community members. The rhythmical drumming, chanting, and singing will help him to reenact his feelings, help him to become the prey, by behaving and being like it. The traditional chanters and dancers possessed the ability to enter into the spirit of the hunter and prey. Visualization, and possibly the trancelike state of the person then seems to say that man, animal, and spirit become one. It means that as we imagine, we cannot separate ourselves from whatever we are picturing.

Shamans, men or women, who have had a profound experience hunting or who have seen an everyday activity in a different or comical way will turn it into song and dance. The Eskimo Orpingalik stated that, "Songs are thoughts, sung out with the breath when people are moved by great forces and ordinary speech no longer suffices . . . it will happen that the words we use will come of themselves. When the words we want to use shoot up themselves—we get a new song" (qtd. in Halifax 1979). The "enlightened wisdom" of a spiritual being seems to express itself without the conscious effort of the recipient, the person through whom it is speaking. All it requires is that the person be willing to be the vehicle for expression.

The Yupiaq refer to "distant time" as *nunam qainga mamkillrani* or 'when the earth's crust was thin,' at which time strange things happened (Nelson 1983). It was easy for human beings or animals to change form, so that a person could become a bird, bear, or seal, or an animal could take the human form to communicate with people. Or a small rock could be placed on a human's body, as when being pursued by a bear, and it would appear that the human being disappeared, but in its place was a boulder. The animal might ask, "What happened to the man? Where did this boulder come from?" But after looking it over, it would eventually leave. The small stone that many Yupiaq people still carry is known as an *iinruk*, or 'medicine' for want of a better term. It is the protector. That word today has also come to represent pharmaceutical prescriptions given by modern doctors.

A major figure in Yupiaq mythology is the Raven. As with other Native American stories of the Raven, He is a trickster and has supernatural powers, but often suffers from frailties, not unlike the human being. The Ellam Yua is rarely if ever mentioned, but Its existence is acknowledged, and It is everywhere. However, the

Raven's accomplishments, antics, and misadventures proliferate in myths and legends. He is profound, clever, and ludicrous all at the same time. With a creator such as He, how can the Yupiaq ever feel guilt about being in this world? As long as they are willing to live with the Yupiaq by-laws of life, admonitions, and rules for behavior, they should have no fear but to live life to the best of their ability.

The Raven is credited with many accomplishments. The Milky Way that is visible on a clear night represents the tracks of the Raven as He traveled across the sky on His snowshoes. Our ancestors have told us to acknowledge and recognize them. One story has Him living on Qaluyaat (Nelson Island). The place that He lives in is on an inlet. One day He hunts and is successful. He has his wife go to butcher the catch. While she is on the ice butchering His catch, a break opens, and the ice floats away. The Raven learns of this, runs into the house, gathers loose earth, carries it, and runs out of the house and throws it into the inlet. This earth that He threw became low-lying mountains on the Qaluyaat.

Another story has Raven's daughter having her first menstruation. It was the practice in those days to separate the menstruating daughter from others. He has her sitting on a mound on a mountain a short distance from His house. This site of her menstruation became the site of ocher, reddish in color. Only the women were allowed to go to this place to get ocher for natural coloring of ornaments.

It is said that the Raven's doorway was visible at one time, but no one has gone there to see whether it and other signs still exist. It is said that His door cover was visible in the rock and that His forefinger imprints were discernible in the rock. Story knife designs were also present. Somewhere above Tununermiut (Tununak), the Raven was said to have tried ice-picking a tunnel to the ocean bottom so that hunters who met disaster would be able to return to the land through this tunnel. However, His pick broke before He could complete His task. He left the broken pick, saying, "I'll just put it here, and if any one of my descendants finds it, he will become wealthy." No one has yet found the broken pick.

The Yupiaq worldview, including the myths, legends, and stories, reflects the interconnectedness of all things in this world as bestowed by the Ellam Yua flowing through and being in everything. The Yupiaq rituals and ceremonies enable them to recognize their own uniqueness as human beings and the interconnectedness of all. The Yupiaq worldview traditionally gave its practitioners a way to live a satisfying and harmonious life. It has been shown by current research that our thoughts, beliefs, and expectations largely influence our well-being and our immune systems. The Yupiaq worldview enabled the Yupiaq people to be in control of their lives. Their traditional subsistence way of life required a physically fit body bolstered by natural foods. The Yupiaq people had to maintain a positive mental attitude to make a living and a life in an unpredictable environment. This meant releasing all negative thoughts from the mind by participating in steam baths, singing and dancing, talking with others, playing games, spending time in silence with one's own thoughts, learning to relax, and visualizing a good life. Their wants and needs were limited and thus their possessions as well, making their life manageable. The Yupiaq people laughed easily and had a well-developed sense of humor. No matter how tough things might get, the laughter helped them adjust to the new situation and not take themselves and life too seriously. All of these produced a quality of life satisfying in Yupiaq eyes.

Alaska Native Lifeways and Education

Since the inception of modern education in the villages, the curricula, policies, textbooks, language of instruction, and administration have been in conflict with the Native cultural systems. The modern public schools are not made to accommodate differences in worldviews (Locust 1988), but to impose another culture—their own (Berger, Berger, & Kellner 1974). This has had a confusing effect on the Native students. Alienation and identity crisis among the youth and their continual search for meaning are conditions of Native life today (Berger, Berger, & Kellner 1974:94). New images of modernity collide with traditional symbols, values and beliefs.

From the time of first contact between Western and Native societies, there has been a clash of worldviews. The Native peoples were told in no uncertain terms that their ways of life were inferior and that these would have to be changed to fit the newcomers' values and ways. As a result, the Native peoples suffered a loss of control over their daily lives (Darnell 1979; Hopson 1977; Yupiktak Bista 1977). Education was one of the first colonial institutions. Colonial administrators began to plan the fate of a people of which they had not been a part. They considered their ways superior, and in pursuit of their own imperial needs, they disregarded the needs of the Native people.

These early educational systems were not structured to give knowledge and skills to Native youngsters for service to their people and country, but rather to give service to the colonial government. It was the colonialists' intent to inculcate the colonial values and to foster docility and obsequious service to the state (Darnell 1979). The colonial system left in the previously self-directed Native peoples' consciousnesses a sense of subordination, confusion and debilitation, a fate shared by indigenous and colonized people around the world (Egede 1985; Kirkness 1977; Nyerere 1968; Okoko 1987; Omari 1990).

Most secondary schools for Alaska Natives were located in urban areas with dormitories for youngsters coming in from rural areas (Darnell 1979; Pratt 1976). The rationale behind residential schools was to facilitate the shift away from their languages and lifeways and to separate them from the influence of their parents. For this and other reasons, the schools' classrooms have often been battlefields for Native children (Chrisjohn, Towson, & Peters 1988). Many were too young to cope with a new environment, and their removal from family, friends, and community contributed to numerous psychosocial problems in later life. It was a cataclysmic experience from which Native people are still struggling to recover (Napoleon 1991).

As the Western world encroached on Alaska Native territories, the posture of Native people was not unlike that of other Native Americans, to attempt to "take the best from the white man's knowledge by acquiring a formal education in the field of choice, while affirming the Indian spiritual worldview" (Martin 1991:28). However, it is apparent that there is a significant contrast between the Western educational system and Native worldviews. The former is formulated to study and analyze objectively learned facts to predict and assert control over the forces of nature. But Alaska Native people have their own ways of looking at and relating to the world, the universe, and to each other. These ways have seldom been recognized by the expert educators of the Western world, whose educational system is instituted to inculcate Western knowledge and values.

Recently, however, many Natives as well as non-Natives are recognizing that the Western system does not always mesh well with the Native worldview, and new approaches are being devised. In this book it is my intention to contribute to our understanding of the relationship between Native worldviews and Western education, so that we can devise a system of education for all that respects the philosophical foundation provided by Native cultural tradition. How, then, have that cultural tradition and worldview been affected as a result of prolonged contact with the people and institutions of Western society? And what role does and can the educational system play in ameliorating the consequences of that contact? These are the questions to which the remainder of the book will be addressed, focusing on the experiences of a particular Yupiaq community and the cultural region in which it is situated.

Chapter 2

Akiak and the Yupiit Nation

The Yupiit Nation

The focus of this study is the Yupiit Nation and its school system. This tribally governed nation is located on the Kuskokwim River and is composed of three Yupiaq villages—Akiachak, Akiak, and Tuluksak. Their populations range from 275 to 500. The largest village is Akiachak, which is the seat of government for the nation. It is located approximately seventeen miles downriver from Akiak, which is the community in which the fieldwork was centered.

Ann Fienup-Riordan (1990) has stated that many Westerners were doubtful as to whether the Yupiit Nation would work at all when the three villages reconstituted themselves in the early 1980s, because from a Western perspective they lacked the necessary bureaucratic system with tiers of high-paid, well-titled workers. Now the surrounding villages that make up the Association of Village Council Presidents are considering a tribal government for the whole region. The three small villages defied the federal and state governments and faced the uncertainty of conflicting laws and a reluctant bureaucratic system to establish their own tribal government (Fienup-Riordan 1990).

Shortly after Alaska acquired statehood in 1959, the Yupiaq of the villages of Akiak, Akiachak, and Tuluksak had watched their

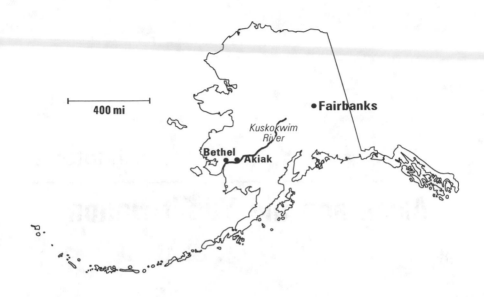

400 mi

•**Fairbanks**

*Kuskokwim
River*

Bethel •Akiak

Alaska

hegemony slip further and further away from their villages. Yupiaq culture was not being used to enhance and strengthen the Yupiaq way of life. As long as control was in the hands of the state and the school district, the Yupiaq people felt that no change would occur. It was the wish of the villagers that education reflect the culture of the village. The passage by the U.S. Congress of the Alaska Native Claims Settlement Act of 1971 further complicated matters, as it altered the villages' control over land and resources. Subsequent congressional action, the Alaska National Interest Lands and Conservation Act (1980), attempted to reestablish certain Native rights, but many questions remain, and different interpretations of the law abound. Each special-interest group attempts to interpret and translate the law to support its own views.

To illustrate the complexity of the current legal status of Yupiaq people, the following excerpt is taken verbatim from the testimony of the chairman of the Yupiit Nation Council of Elders on April 13, 1992. It addresses many of the concerns and problems as experienced by the Yupiit Nation:

The issue of self-government by the residential indigenous peoples is the important goal of the Yupiit Nation and its member villages. Although there is no clear policy towards indigenous self-government authority from the federal and state government perspective, the movement to revitalize indigenous governments is the strongest within our people in the Southwestern part of Alaska.

The Yupiit Nation was created by Resolution 84-07-01 of the Pinariuq Conference conducted by the Inuit governments of Akiachak, Akiak and Tuluksak on the 6th of July 1984, at Akiachak Native Community.

The purposes of the Yupiit Nation were identified as (1) to strengthen unity among the Yupiit of Southwest Alaska, (2) to promote Yupiit rights and interests on the local, national and international levels of policy development effecting the Yupiit, (3) to ensure Yupiit participation in political, economical and social institutions which we deem relevant, (4) to promote greater self-sufficiency of the Yupiit in Southwest Alaska, (5) to ensure the endurance and growth of the Yupiit culture and societies for both present and future generations, (6) to promote long-term management and use of non-renewable resources in western Alaska and incorporate such resources in the present and future development of Yupiit economies, taking into account other Yupiit interests.

The United States government experimented with Alaska Natives by settling land claims with corporations rather than with indigenous governments. The Alaska Native Claims Settlement Act provided 44 million acres of lands to all indigenous residents of Alaska and paid close to a billion dollars for the rest of our traditional homelands and extinguishment of certain rights. For that reason, the Yupiit Nation views the Alaska Native Claims Settlement Act as a genocidal and termination act because of non-involvement of our children born after the settlement of lands. Attempts have been made to provide a transfer to tribes from corporations and to include children in the settlement in the so-called 1991 amendments to ANCSA. Although the amendments addressed indigenous youth, there is no guarantee that they will benefit.

The Alaska Native Claims Settlement Act forced the indigenous residents to change from hunters and gatherers to corporate businessmen in a very short period of time. Many of the business corporations are facing bankruptcy. Because these corporations own the traditional homelands, the lands are in jeopardy of being lost forever. I have to say that some of the village corporations are also doing well and are providing limited benefit to their shareholders.

Because the corporations are visible in all indigenous communities, the tribes' economic rights are almost non-visible to almost non-existent. Because of statehood, many of the indigenous communities are organized as governmental entities or subdivisions of state government. Although the indigenous governments do exist, the municipal governments are assuming responsibilities on a village level for both indigenous and non-indigenous peoples.

Because of the emergence of non-indigenous governments and businesses, the way of life of the indigenous residents of Alaska is fast disappearing. Unless people on a grass-roots level evaluate their priorities through revitalization of their traditional governments, a way of life will be lost forever.

By involving ourselves in the Indigenous Peoples Preparatory Meeting at the Palais des Nations July 24 to July 28, 1989 for the drafting of the Universal Declaration on the Rights of Indigenous Peoples and our presentation on our developments to the Working Group shows our support and the importance of the adoption by the United Nations of the Universal Declaration on the Rights of Indigenous Peoples.

It is essential that this declaration of the universal rights of indigenous peoples be adopted because many of the principles do not exist for the indigenous peoples of Alaska due to lack of clear policy from the United States government.

Two specific examples are the right to ownership of subsurface lands by the villages and individual indigenous peoples of Alaska. The subsurface lands are owned by the regional ANCSA corporations and not the villages. Individual indigenous peoples who own land allotments also do not enjoy subsurface rights and cannot develop them even though the same federal laws are used to grant land ownership to individual Alaska Natives as for the Indians in the continental United States.

We feel that through the use of the indigenous governments, our customs, cultures, languages, and histories can be preserved and flourish into the future and benefit the world community in better understanding of each other's cultures.

One of the first areas in which the Yupiit Nation asserted its rights was education. A board of education was established under the

Tribal Council, and a contract to run their own school was arranged under the federal Indian Self-Determination and Educational Assistance Act (1975). Lacking formally educated and certificated people, however, the board has had to hire personnel from outside the region. These outsiders are usually non-Native. The degree to which the wishes and hopes of the Native board are reflected in the schooling and curricula of the Yupiit School District remains a question (Madsen 1983). In Fienup-Riordan's estimation, "Many non-Natives view the Yupiit Nation's attempt at political revitalization as a contradiction in terms. How, they ask, can Eskimos 'revitalize' traditional governance and law ways when 'contained anarchy' characterized past political organization? They reject out of hand the Yupiaq bid to take control, saying that with no history of chiefs or political institutions, the Yupiaq people will be unable to govern properly. The Yupiit Nation (they believe) can be successful only insofar as it effectively mirrors non-Eskimo models of governance" (1990:195). To me, this thinking represents a bias on the part of the non-Native people. The contained-anarchy notion was first used by Wendell Oswalt in his studies of Yupiaq people (1963).

In an effort to counteract the erroneous views indicated above, the Tribal Council contracted with Fienup-Riordan to investigate the features of traditional law and government used by Yupiaq people at the time of contact. In her report, she identifies several core values of Yupiaq people and their code of conduct (1990). Some of the relevant Yupiaq words are: *qaneryaraat*, 'oral teachings'; *alerquutet*, 'laws or instructions'; and *inerquutet*, 'admonitions or warnings.' She goes on to say that "the traditional system of laws was so elaborate and highly structured that it defies characterization as 'informal' or 'primitive.'" She quotes Yupiaq elder Paul John (1930-): "We have had laws from our very beginnings. The *kass'aq* [white man] thinks we have none because, unlike his, ours are not contained in books. Like the kass'aq we have strong laws; the strength of our law is no different from his. Our grandparents repeatedly told the law so we could learn" (cited in Fienup-Riordan 1990:205). With these ideas in mind, the Yupiaq people of Akiak and the Yupiit Nation are now working toward the development of an educational system for their children that is Yupiaq in as many respects as possible, including the rules of law and behavior under which it operates.

Akiak on the Kuskokwim

The Yupiaq Eskimo village of Akiak is located about 35 miles upriver from Bethel, the goods-and-services distribution hub of the southwestern Alaska tundra. Akiak currently has a population of 285. The older Yupiaq people recall how, during the early 1900s, Akiak was the regional center of the Kuskokwim River Delta. They refer the inquisitive visitor to photographs of a hospital, a sawmill, and many large gardens. Bethel, a community of about 5,000, has since become the center of transportation, commerce, and communication in the region. The Bethel port is capable of accommodating ocean-going barges and fish processors, and the airport elevation is above flood level—advantages that Akiak does not possess.

There are various sources of historical information about Akiak, such as Erik Madsen's unpublished dissertation of 1983, several books by Moravian missionaries and various scholars (Collier, J. 1973; Collier, M. 1979; Fienup-Riordan 1990; Henkelman & Vitt 1985; Oswalt 1990; Schwalbe 1951), and elders from the villages. At one time, Akiak was a thriving kick-off center for reindeer herders as well as miners. It even had a hospital and several trading stores. It was a segregated village, with Native people living on the west side of the river where Akiak is presently located and whites living in the now-deserted east side of the river.

An eleven-bed hospital constructed in Akiak by the Alaska Native Medical Service opened in 1918. In the succeeding years of its operation, it suffered from recruiting doctors who were ill-suited to the environment and the people that it served. After two very unsatisfactory experiences with two doctors, the hospital had to close its doors in 1933–34 (Oswalt 1990).

The first Moravian Church was built and dedicated on September 8, 1913. My great-grandfather and grandfather both became associated with the early missionaries: "The work at Akiak was more than encouraging. Helper Kawagleg was working diligently among the people and most of the village was expressing an interest in joining the Church" (Henkelman & Vitt 1985:211).

The Presbyterian missionary, Sheldon Jackson, in his efforts to help the Yupiaq people, conceived of and implemented, with the aid of the federal government, the introduction of reindeer to the Delta. By the early 1930s the reindeer industry was well established locally, though most of the animals at the time belonged to the government-recruited Lapps and whites, not to the Eskimos.

Several large herds were located in the region. About 35,000 reindeer reportedly were owned by Eskimo and non-Native Akiak residents, 5,000 grazed in the vicinity of Tuluksak, and 3,000 belonged to the Bethel herd. In the late 1930s, the number was reported to be nearly the same, although the herds were more widely distributed. The following was reported in the minutes of a Reindeer Herders' gathering in Akiak: "The whole group of herders, with their wives and families attended, discussing the relation between apprentice and herd owners, the relative rights of dogs and reindeer, the care of the herding dogs and the care of the reindeer." (Henkelman & Vitt 1985:310–1). Incredible as it may seem, by 1946 only 600 animals remained in a single herd at Akiak, and shortly thereafter they had disappeared (Oswalt 1990). Many factors may have contributed to the demise of the reindeer, among them governmental interference in management, predators, and perhaps the reluctance of the Yupiaq people to become herders.

Madsen (1983) mentions that the river provided a means of transportation and served as a provider of food for the villagers. According to Oswalt, early explorers may have found the Delta inhospitable, "but the Eskimos living inland found the river to be a great and highly dependable provider. They relied on fish, especially salmon, as their primary staple. In addition, they depended heavily on the upland tundra as hunting and trapping grounds. Whites settled among the Eskimos to transform them into consumers of Western products as well as Christians, to educate them in schools, and to administer varied social, economic, and political programs intended to change the quality of their lives" (1990:11). The Akiak village school was founded by the Moravian missionaries in 1911, almost a decade before the establishment of other village schools, except for Bethel, which was founded in 1886 (Oswalt 1990).

Akiak possesses a tribal form of government, organized under the federal Indian Reorganization Act (IRA) of 1934. Exercising its tribal government authority, Akiak took the initiative in 1980 to contract the operation of the local elementary school from the Bureau of Indian Affairs (BIA). Public Law 93-638, the Indian Self-Determination and Educational Assistance Act (1975), was the enabling legislation under which Akiak sought the authority to run its own school. "Through grants and contracts, the Act encourages tribes to assume administrative responsibility for federally funded programs that were designed for their benefit and that previously were administered by employees of the Bureau of Indian Affairs and

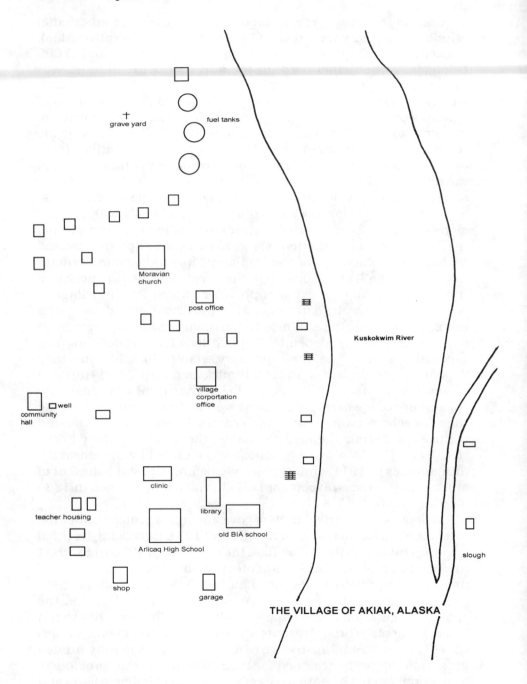

grave yard

fuel tanks

Moravian church

post office

Kuskokwim River

village corportation office

community hall

well

clinic

teacher housing

library

old BIA school

Arlicaq High School

shop

garage

slough

THE VILLAGE OF AKIAK, ALASKA

the United States Indian Health Service" (American Indian Lawyer Training Program 1988:15). After a long and difficult struggle, the application for the IRA tribal government to serve as the contractor for the local elementary school was finally approved in 1980 (Madsen 1983). At the same time, the state-funded Lower Kuskokwim Regional School District established and operated a high school in the village independent of the contract school. The school was operated by the village under contract with the Bureau of Indian Affairs for five years, until the state of Alaska recognized the three Yupiit Nation villages as an independent school district in 1985, making them eligible for regular state funding. At that point, the elementary and high schools were taken over under the banner of the new Yupiit School District.

Akiak and the Modern World

Were my great-great-grandmother alive today, she would be astounded by the changes that have been wrought to her homeland by the influx of Western institutions and technology. She would be inquisitive about the research I am doing with the concomitant Western knowledge and methodologies that I have garnered over the years. She would quietly query me about this new knowledge and its applications in the Yupiaq world. She probably would not come out directly with the observation that much of what I know is useless knowledge but likely would remain skeptical and hold that what I have learned from my scientific training is second-rate knowledge that is not particularly reliable for solving village problems.

Be that as it may, Western science and technology have had an enormous impact in the villages. "Impact" infers passive acceptance of new things, which often has been the case with the Yupiaq. A few resisted education and acceptance of modern tools and implements, but the majority did not. My grandmother's parents would not allow her to go to school, saying that she would get dumb. By "dumb" I think they meant that she would lose her values and traditions and begin to live another way of life. Much of the traditional knowledge and experiences of the Yupiaq were adapted to the environment and learned through the tasks of daily life in that environment. These were known to work down through the millennia, with slight changes that resulted from climactic permutations and the resultant changes in flora and fauna.

Complete and sudden change would mean destruction of the Yupiaq worldview. However, after some initial resistance during early contact, and especially after the loss of leaders and shamans during the great influenza epidemic of the early 1900s (Napoleon 1991), the Yupiaq became more receptive to innovation. Science and technology continue to be the conveyors of change in the Yupiaq region.

Most homes are very well furnished with a modern flare. Clothing is predominantly Western, with only the most traditional people sometimes wearing a pair of Yupiaq boots, commonly called mukluks. Food consumption depends to a large extent on the income of the household, with store-bought food alternated or mixed with Native foods. It has been estimated by Nunam Kliutsiti, a regional resource-monitoring organization, that on the average, food consumption in the Delta consists of about 50 percent Native foods and the other half outside foods. This indicates that the Yupiaq people have been adapting to a cash economy for quite some time.

Since the time of early contact when Arlicaq (ca.1863), a respected traditional chief, moved from the east side of the Kuskokwim river to the present site of Akiak and built his sod house, there has been tremendous change. No longer are the villagers living in semisubterranean sod houses of Yupiaq design. These traditional houses were heat efficient, with cold air traps at the entrance and openings above the door to allow for natural air conditioning. The materials were of nature—driftwood or local trees, sod, grass, and wooden planks. These houses belonged to nature.

There are several old timber-constructed houses still standing and in use that probably date back to the time that Akiak had a sawmill, but the majority of homes today are frame houses built by funds from the federal Department of Housing and Urban Development (HUD) or the Alaska State Housing Authority. All building materials are imported from the "South Forty-eight." The new homes are built on pilings and suspended above the ground because of flooding and permafrost problems.

Older homes have a kitchen stove that serves as a cooking source as well as heat for the building. The newer ones have an elaborate furnace and heat delivery system, an enclosed system in which a heated glycol mixture is pumped through piping to various parts of the building. The furnace is an oil-fired system controlled by a thermostat. All new houses have a divided interior configuration with bedrooms and a combination living/dining section and storage space. Villagers often complain that the new houses fall apart in a matter of two to four years. The maintenance cost of these homes, including heating and electricity, is exorbitant. The occupants pay whatever they can afford to the Association of Village Council Presidents, Inc. (AVCP), a regional tribal organization whose responsibility it is to construct, maintain, and oversee payments on the housing.

Many of the newest homes built during the oil money glut of the early 1980s have an individual septic tank and well, providing running water and flush toilets. Older homes have "honey buckets" for human waste, which are usually emptied into the backyard. Garbage disposal poses another problem imported from the outside world, with all of its nonbiodegradable packaging. Sewage and garbage are endemic problems in the villages. Most village sites are barely above sea level, thus causing additional storage problems and health hazards.

Many homes have modern appliances, including refrigerators, toasters, microwave ovens, electric or oil-fired stoves, freezers of varying sizes, and many other items the families now consider essential. The television set and VCR are often among the most prominent items in the home and often serve as the center of activity. Many homes have Nintendo games, which people of every age enjoy playing. Sometimes the TV is left on all day, whether anyone is watching or not.

Research on the impact of television in rural Alaska has indicated that this outside element alone can cause the cultural lens to become astigmatic in young, developing minds, when a very channelized version of outside cultural values and traditions are seen, most often blurred or distorted (Forbes 1984). A constant barrage of television programs is beamed into the villages. These establish pseudorealities for the young, and the advertising links up with the desperate expectations for a better life, and because Native people have an unsophisticated sense of deception by modern communications (which is most often one-way), they think they need and want more. They mimic what they see on TV, try to dress like its characters, have fun and recreation with electronic gadgets, long to be beautiful white people with beautiful homes, and adopt the mannerisms and language of another world without realizing that these are inimical to their traditional way of life. This causes confusion among the young and, eventually, disillusionment with the Yupiaq way of life.

Most homes have telephones and/or a citizens band radio. The latter is left on most of the time, so that individual messages can be relayed or collective village messages delivered through it. It is used to announce the arrival of a dignitary or a meeting that will take place. The radios are often carried on boats, snow machines, and vehicles for emergency purposes or just to stay in touch. The post office employs one person and is a very important source of shipping and receiving packages and mail. As in other communities, there is a blight of unwanted and unsolicited mail.

Upon changeover from the federal Bureau of Indian Affairs–funded school to the state-funded Yupiit School District, the old BIA school had to be brought up to state codes. The old school was a very substantially built school and after refurbishing is a highly functional building. In addition, a new school was built to accommodate local high school students. It is a replica of most of the village high schools that were built as the result of a lawsuit against the state in the mid-1970s. This case required the state to build high schools in villages where there were at least eight students of elementary age and one or more high school age students. So, in the 1970s and 1980s the state went on a building frenzy with the dollars available from oil revenues. The design was similar for each with the exception of a half-, three-quarter, or full-size gymnasium, depending on the size of the school. Inadequate attention to operational efficiency considerations caused an inordinate portion of the school budget to go toward future maintenance, electricity, and fuel. The equipment is so complicated that experts have to be flown in sometimes from the district central office or from Anchorage to make repairs. The biggest share of the budget goes for teacher and administrative salaries. Of the nine teachers in Akiak, two are Alaska Native and the principal is part American Indian. A number of local Native people are employed as teacher aides, cooks and cook's helpers, maintenance personnel, secretaries, and bilingual aides. The school is the biggest employer in the village.

About seven families own dog teams, which are used more for recreational purposes than for hunting and trapping. Some owners combine training dogs with putting meat on the table by using them for subsistence hunting, but the predominant use is for dog-sled racing. Most transportation is by aluminum boats with outboard motors, snow machines, three- and four-wheelers, and some four-wheel drive cars and pickups. The cost of outboard motors varies from $1,000 to $6,500, and the aluminum boats range from $900 to $11,000, depending on size. All-terrain vehicles and snow machines range from $1,500 to $7,000.

Adding to the accumulated pollution in the village are many cannibalized machines of all sorts—cars, trucks, aluminum boats, outboard motors, three- and four-wheelers, washing machines, electric generators, heavy equipment, an old fire engine, sundry wrappings, and numerous other discarded modern things. The village dump is overflowing, and there is no sewage disposal except for a few homes that have running water and flush toilets. Waste disposal is a big problem.

Many boats with motors still attached are left on the river shore during the winter. This is quite a change from the time that I grew up, when it was expected that one would take good care of the boat and motor. This meant making sure the boat was placed on the riverbank, overturned, and the motor stored in the smokehouse or under the boat. This recent throwaway mentality treats such equipment as merely a technological, easily replaceable appendage.

There are two locally owned stores, a village Native corporation office, and a community center that houses the tribal and municipal employees as well as the laundry. The village corporation runs the oil and gas service, a small store that sells oil products, and a recreational and sport fishing operation on the Kiseralik River. State, federal, and private funds are used to operate these ventures. A number of small air-taxi services take passengers, mail, and freight from Akiak to Bethel or vice versa.

There are perhaps eight miles of road in Akiak. It is a very expensive undertaking to make a road in the river delta. The gravel must be barged in from up-river gravel bars. First the tundra and brush are removed by a tractor, then a base of gravel poured and compacted. Then it is a matter of pouring more gravel on top of each compacted layer to build it up a foot or two above ground level. The airport is one of the most important facilities and is maintained with equipment and funds from the state department of transportation. Enough funds are allocated to provide for a small tractor, a garage for it, maintenance, and an operator. It is his responsibility to keep the airport serviceable by smoothing it of potholes in the summer and keeping it plowed of snow in the winter. Responding to snow and winds during the winter occupies a lot of his time.

The city has a fire engine, but it does not run; the earth-moving truck is also not functional. Heavy equipment must be barged in to do construction work, such as building the electric generator house, during which heavy timbers had to be moved and placed. Once the building's foundation was completed, the generator had to be lifted into place. All this required heavy machinery. For

anything major, such as a construction project, not only must the needed equipment be transported to the site but also heavy equipment operators. Locals provide the manual labor. Given the complexity and rapidity of the changes that have taken place in villages such as Akiak and among the Yupiaq people as a whole, many cultural, educational, and technological adaptations have been necessary.

Consequences of Adaptation

The encroachment of Western civilization in the Yupiaq world changed a people that did not seek changing. The Yupiaq peoples' systems of education, governance, spirituality, economy, being, and behavior were very much in conformity with their philosophy of life and provided for harmonious living. The people were satisfied with the quality of their life and felt that their technology was in accord with it. The culture- and nature-mediated technology was geared to a sustainable level of self-sufficiency.

The people in general were sufficiently content with their lifestyle that they did not readily accept Western education and religions when the first envoys of the dominant society set foot in their land. Western knowledge and technological might did not bring the Yupiaq people to compliance—rather it was the incomprehensible diseases that decimated the people. A great number of elders, mothers and/or fathers, shamans, and children succumbed to these new diseases. Whole villages were wiped out. The missionaries began to open orphanages and schools for the newly dislocated exiles in their own land. A hospital was located in Akiak, and the Moravian Church established a "Children's Home" a short distance up river. The Federal Bureau of Education established "contract schools" with religious organizations. Money was paid to these organizations to establish schools and pay for the missionary teachers. The children were taught a new language (English) along with new knowledge and skills to become servants to the newcomers' needs and as laborers for newly established businesses. The Compulsory School Attendance Law was enacted, requiring families to remain in one location for many months of the year,

◀Boats and motors buried in winter snow on riverbank at Akiak.

thus ending the Native peoples' practice of moving from place to place according to the seasons. The restrictive law initiated a twelve-year sentence given all Native children to attend school. Today, that sentence has increased to thirteen, including kindergarten. This has greatly reduced the freedom of people to be who they are, to learn traditional values, and to live in harmony with their environment. It has meant that the families and children no longer experience the great freedom of earlier times.

The Yupiit School District does not require that the Yupiaq children learn their own languages and lifeways, but rather they are expected to learn a foreign language and the related humanities and sciences. The majority of teachers are from the outside world and have little or no knowledge of the people with whom they are going to be working. To the people in Akiak, these are an immigrant people with a different way of being, thinking, behaving and doing from the Yupiaq. Few teachers recognize that the indigenous Yupiaq are not like other European ethnic groups, such as the Irish, French, or Italians, who have chosen to leave their homeland. By not teaching the Yupiaq youngsters their own language and way of doings things, the classroom teachers are telling them that their language, knowledge, and skills are of little importance. The students begin to think of themselves as being less than other people. After all, they are expected to learn through a language other than their own, to learn values that are in conflict with their own, and to learn a "better" way of seeing and doing things. They are taught the "American Dream" which, in their case, is largely unattainable, without leaving behind who they are.

The messages from the school, the media, and other representations of Western society present Akiak students with an unreal picture of the outside world, as well as a distorted view of their own, which leads to a great deal of confusion for students over who they are and where they fit in the world. This loss of Yupiaq identity leads to guilt and shame at being Yupiaq. The resultant feelings of hurt, grief and pain are locked in the mind to emerge as depression, which is further reinforced by the fear of failure in school, by ridicule from non-Natives, and by the loss of their spirituality. The question now is: How do we counteract the depression, hopelessness, and despair that derive from the unfulfilled promises of the modern world, and what role can schooling and education play in this effort? To address this question, it will be necessary to take a closer look at how traditional education and Western schooling have fit into the lives of the Yupiaq people.

Chapter 3

Yupiaq Science, Technology, and Survival

Yupiaq science and technology are mediated by both nature and culture. Fritzof Capra (1984) defines technology as "the application of human knowledge to the solution of practical problems." This the Yupiaq have done to an exemplary degree, except perhaps in the last fifty years. In the distant past, they concentrated on what may be thought of as "soft" technology, whereby the making of tools and implements, construction of shelter, means of governance, conflict resolution, and so forth, were done with as little harm to the natural and supernatural worlds as possible. The shamans were the central figures for communications with the spiritual and natural worlds. They were the ones to expound on what was appropriate or not in Yupiaq dealings with the earth. Their consciousness and knowledge determined their built environment as well. Their housing technology was made to disturb the environment as little as possible. Their transport and hunting and trapping technology made use of natural materials that were recyclable and did not offend the creatures whose lives they had to take to live. They took extensive precautions in their practices to ensure continued life of the creatures they depended upon. They practiced a set of values that gave meaning to and guided their actions in all aspects of their existence. In this chapter, those values, meanings, and actions and some of their consequences will be examined in greater detail.

Science and Mathematics from a Yupiaq Perspective

At a gathering of several Yupiaq elders, I asked them to consider ways in which we might improve the school curriculum. In the course of the discussion, the five Yupiaq speakers spent considerable time trying to define the Western notions of "mathematics" and "science" in Yupiaq thought and terms. Previous to this, they had been talking about the Yupiaq ancient ways as being bountiful and prescribed to maintain a balance with nature. The elders mentioned that the young people of today are not being taught Yupiaq and were thus losing the knowledge of their ancestors. They said that the young are taught the culture of the Western world in high school, and then those graduates who stay in the village cannot fit very well into the ways of the village. They have been alienated from the traditional Native ways, looking upon them as being "primitive" and "useless." Yet these young high-school graduates, who grow in numbers every year, must still live with their parents and relatives, contributing little to their own support. They tax the already burgeoning need for housing, recreational facilities, welfare, subsistence resources, social and psychological aid, health services, suitable land, and jobs.

The Yupiaq elders continued and said that those few who do go on to higher education often find their education useless upon return to the village. The job market is so small and the things learned are not necessarily suited to the village lifestyle. They spoke in sympathy and empathy, especially for the young men who do acquire a Western education and, as a result, find it difficult to return to the village after an experience away from home, with all its concomitant problems of homesickness, limited financial support, and ethnic tensions. In the process, they unlearn what few Native values and ways they had learned in the village. In essence they become emigrants and exiles from their own language, values, traditions, and homeland. It is difficult to try to live in two worlds without adequate bridges between them. The elders' conclusion was that the Yupiaq students should be taught both the Western and Yupiaq cultures in the schools, in a way that recognized their essential interconnectedness as occupants of the same land.

In the elders' words, the land and the water provided the

resources that served as the livelihood of our Yupiaq ancestors. The plants and the animals of the land and the fishes and mammals of the waters were the sources of the ancestors' lives. They lived prosperously on their own terms and had few worries. Their lives were quiet, with a minimum of stress, and thus the Yupiaq people were kind and polite toward other people. They were very conscious of family ties and the bond that existed among them. Through sharing of food, thoughts, and service they developed and maintained this strong tie. They extended this thoughtfulness to others in places both far and near. "Love thy neighbor as thyself" was brought to fruition in their lives. When there was a need, help was given freely, without need for payment.

With respect to education, the elders agreed that if the students were required to learn both ways, then they would be able to say, "I have learned that my ancestors lived this way, and since I don't have a job, I will continue to live following the methods and livelihood practiced by my ancestors." Learning both ways, the graduates would not be ignorant of the options available to them and be comfortable in using either way.

The elders' discussion of the definition of mathematics focused on the Yupiaq word *Cuqtaariyaraq*, 'the process of measuring.' The other definitions that were considered reflect further abstractions of their thinking processes as applied to one who uses mathematics. These included "someone who is astute and perceptive"; "an expert evaluator"; "an expert assessor"; "someone who evaluates something, mentally assessing the feasibility and coming pretty close to the estimate"; "becoming good at calculating"; and "becoming good at visualizing." Finally, they agreed that the best Yupiaq definition of mathematics would be "the process of measuring and estimating in time and space."

In ancient times, it was not important to measure things precisely. It was much more convenient to use commonsense measurements and estimations. For example, it was not necessary to count the number of fish caught but to look at the space filled and compare it to space filled in times past to judge whether one has enough to last the year. The need for more precise and complex mathematics to divide the land for individual ownership was not necessary either, since the land and waters were collectively owned.

Trying to define "science" elicited the following ideas from the elders, though no corresponding Yupiaq word was identified: "trying to know," "trying to understand," "trying to grasp the origin," "trying to find the source," "the process of understanding," "way to try to understand by process of elimination," "a process that is the science of life," and "a process of forseeing and predicting the future." In the course of the discussion they made comments such as this: "and this is what our ancestors have said; they've said not to pollute the land. They've said that if we're not careful with our refuse, some animals, though they were plentiful once, will no longer be around. They were actually foreseeing their future when they told us that." "That's the science of life. We have to take care of our tundra in order to have plenty and have abundant wildlife."

Science is a quest for knowledge to the Yupiaq, as well as the means to live a long and prosperous life. By assessing the physical phenomena of the present and juxtaposing it against past experience, we gain an idea of what the future holds. The Yupiaq ancestors would use their past experiences as examples of how life was to be lived and as lessons to be learned.

Science and Technology
for Survival on the Kuskokwim

Foreseeing what will happen with natural phenomena is based on readily observable causes and effects, but what the future holds for the people or community is not so easily predicted, because there are few cause-effect variables on which to base the prediction. One 67-year-old elder, when asked to try to predict what Akiak would be like in the future, absolutely refused and would not comment on it. She said that this was a "no-no," and that whatever she said may become true or the opposite might happen, as we have no control over the future.

According to the elders, there are many signs that the earth gives to indicate what is going to be available at any particular time. The language, especially with respect to subject and activity, changes slightly during each season to accommodate different weather, flora, and fauna. Nature is the Yupiaq metaphysic.

Weather

Predicting weather was of much importance as a matter of survival in times past. In the present time, all people need to do is turn on the radio or TV to get a prediction of what the weather is expected to be. Only the elders still retain some of the traditional skills of reading the environment to determine what the weather will be in the near future. One elder said that the modern predictions are often wrong because they rely too much on pictures from way above the earth and do not make use of the senses to interpret the indicators provided by the environment. The elders of the past used all their endosomatic sense makers and powers of observation to predict weather. The gatherer-hunter had to have a good idea of weather conditions so that he or she would be prepared. The elders would go out early in the morning to look at the sky. They observed the cloud formations, noticed whether they were light or dark, and compared the different layers of clouds. They did not have technical names for the different kinds of clouds, but they knew what each would indicate to determine the temperature, wind direction and speed, air pressure, and approximately how long that weather condition would persist. Advice given to people when going outdoors was "Don't forget to look and observe the ella (environment/surroundings) out there."

Not only was the person to observe early in the morning, but he or she was to be aware of changes that occured during the day as well. Early morning observances included the clouds, the horizon, and the sun's emergence. By using his or her eyes, the person could begin to understand the weather by studying the ella (sky) and its permutations. The elders made reference to a Yupiaq saying which when translated means, "The ella does not try to surprise people, but usually tells us ahead of time what it is going to do." They go on to say that we of the present do not know or understand ella, so when the weather takes a turn for the worse, we say that the weather has suddenly gone bad. This is exercising our ignorance. Had we been observant, we would have known that the weather was going to change for the worse. So our elders admonish us to begin to use our eyes and learn to recognize the processes of weather change.

A story is told by one of the elders in which an older man was traveling with his younger cousin. The older man looked at the sun and remarked, "I see that ella is about to bow down. Very bad weather is just about to come." There was not a cloud in the sky, so the younger replied, "Sure, you, being just an ordinary person, do you think this gigantic ella will do as you say?" Later that day they portaged over from the campsite to the Kialiq River. As they approached the last bluff, the ella suddenly "bowed down," and wind-driven heavy snow began to fall. They had to stop and make shelter because the snow was so thick that they could not see the end of their boat. "They say the sun gives you signals. They say that if we are attentive we would learn to recognize its behavior. It gives signals twenty-four hours before it happens." The notion that the sun declares the weather conditions came true for this young man.

There are many environmental signs that the hunter-gatherer learns to read—clouds, sun, moon, northern lights with differing colors and positions in the sky, the stars twinkling, strong winds moving through, and so forth. Those who assess weather by wind are called *angiatuli*, which means to loosen or unravel, to assess, to calculate the mysteries of the weather. These are just a fraction of the indicators that the Yupiaq elders used to tell weather.

The Science of Obtaining Fish

The fish camps from the early times to the present consist of tents for housing, a smokehouse, fish racks, and racks for drying out nets. In recent years, there often is a shell of a house with a framework of two-by-fours covered with plywood. This serves as a family's

Two fish-cutting tables covered with all-weather carpet; fish box at center.

home for the duration of the fishing season. In addition, there may be a small smokehouse used specifically for salmon strips, and very often a plywood steam bath. The people use nylon nets for catching fish. They use steel traps and metal snares for trapping in the winter. Rifles of all calibers and shotguns of all gauges are used for hunting. Fencing materials of all sizes and designs are used for making fish traps. The only traditional Yupiaq tool still extensively used by women is the *uluaq*, a cutting instrument. The size of the uluaq determines whether it is used for cutting large animals or fish or for delicate work.

During the king salmon run in early summer, families carefully fold dried and smoked king salmon slabs and wrap them in plasticized freezer paper. They are then placed in the freezer, where they keep very fresh. Smoked king salmon strips are often vacuum packed, using a vacuum machine with special plastic bags made for that purpose. These are kept in the freezer also. In the 1940s and 1950s, it was the practice to place salmon slabs in wooden barrels to keep them from getting moldy. At that time too it was often the practice to salt fish, but this is not done quite as often now, for it is easier to freeze them. Use of plastic, aluminum, and freezer wrapping materials abounds.

Nature gives signs as to when fish will start up the river. Today, only the elders pay attention to the sign markers of nature and are able to predict when the fish will arrive. Shortly after river break-up, the smelt will come, followed closely by king salmon, then chums and coho. The budding of leaves on alder and willows, the arrival of certain migratory song birds, flowering plants, and water conditions (silty, clear, high water, tides, and so on) are observed to know when a species of fish will be arriving. The elders point out that fish will be most numerous when there is a southerly wind blowing. They say that the wind is pushing the fish up the river. In my observations, growing up in the fish camp for many years, this seems to be true. When one observes the effects of the south wind, there are inordinately high tides, and these make it easier for the fish to swim up the river.

The younger people, on the other hand, know when fish will get to their village by listening to announcements on the radio or TV. They get an idea of how many fish will be available by state Fish and Game estimates (which are very often wrong). The Department of Fish and Game biologists determine when and where the fisherman will engage in commercial or subsistence fishing. They determine when the setnets will be placed and removed. This is

Table 3.1 FISH CAMP ACTIVITIES	
DOMAIN	**INSTRUMENTATION**
Splitting fish	Participant Observation (PO)
Drift netting	PO
Setnetting	PO
Site selection	Interview (I)
Garbage and sewage disposal	PO / I / Document Analysis (DA)
Gardening	PO / I
Housing	PO / I / DA
Boats	PO / I
Heating	PO / I / DA
Power generation	I / DA
Spirituality / values	PO / I
Clothes washing / drying	PO / I
Body cleanliness	PO
Insect control	PO / I
Potable water	PO / I / DA
Fermenting fish	PO / I
Uses of plants, brush and trees	PO / I
Adaptation of tools	PO / I
Tent styles and frames	PO / I
Cooking	PO / I
Smokehouse design and use	PO / I
Means of measurement	PO / I
Science curriculum in school	PO / I / DA
Science teaching practices in school	PO / I

done so that a certain number of fish will escape to their spawning areas. There is no longer need for the villagers to observe and think about the once-vital signs of a subsistence lifestyle. It is being done for them, because the press of a population increase makes regulatory measures necessary. So people set their nets at the assigned hour, even if the times may not be opportune for the best catch.

Setnets are regular nylon fish nets of varying lengths and sizes. They are anchored at one or both ends depending upon whether the net is placed close to the shore or further out in the river, close to a sand bar.

The setting of setnets requires that the individual know the river and its currents. The person learns to look for eddies in the river. This is done by observing the debris of various wood floating on the surface. The action of the wood is carefully watched and, if the detritus moves circularly, it is a good place for the net. The net is checked each day, and twice daily if the fish are running heavy. If the net is left alone for more than a day, the gills of the fish are discolored, and the flesh is soft. To be used for human consumption, the flesh must be firm. The other fish are usually cooked for dog food. Finding a good place for the net requires that the person know about river currents, effects of strong winds, and riverboat wakes. If the anchor on the outer end of the net is light, then a person may have problems with that end drifting downriver or drifting away in a strong storm.

Drifting on the river is the best way for catching most fish, though these days it can be done only during the time prescribed by Fish and Game. In the old days, the best times were when the tide was just beginning its inward or its outward journey. This was noted by placing a stick on the water's edge or by observing the upward current change along the shore. The local people long ago determined that the best drifting areas were places where the river is relatively straight and free of sunken logs and other debris.

Knowing the length of the net, the leader determines where the net should be set by looking at the distance from shore and the position on the river, slows the outboard motor, gives the driving responsibility to the son or brother, and begins to throw out the net. The engine is kept running all the time to keep the net straight as they float down the river. At a certain distance, they decide to pull in the net. Again, the motor is kept running to keep the net straight. One person controls the boat while the other(s) pulls in the net and removes the fish. They are careful to handle the fish by the head, and not the tail, so that little bruising occurs. If they are commercial fishing, they usually have a plastic box and a container of ice from a fish processor, so that as fish are removed from the net, they are carefully placed in the box. Ice is added upon each layer to keep the fish as fresh as possible until they are sold to a fish buyer.

Fish Preparation and Storage for Subsistence

The fish for subsistence use are handled in a different way. Again, the Department of Fish and Game designates certain hours for subsistence fishing, and within the allotted time, the Yupiaq catch as many fish as possible. Upon their return to the fish camp, they unload the boat and put the fish in a four-cornered structure on the ground, at which point the women take over to prepare the fish for drying. Some women prefer to leave the fish for a while, so that they become firm and are easier to split.

The women I interviewed said that king salmon require the most care. There are usually three pails beside the cutting table. One for heads, another for entrails, and the last for fish eggs. Once the head and entrails are removed, they then fillet the fish on both sides with the uluaq, producing a very large slab of salmon meat to be dried and smoked. To facilitate drying, they make lateral cuts about an inch apart. Sometimes these cuts are made approximately at a 45-degree angle to the midpoint; then the angle reverses on the other side, so that when the slab is hung on its midsection, the cuts will open up for better aeration. Some women sprinkle table salt on the salmon to keep flies off. The backbones still contain much flesh that is good for dog food in the winter. Cuts are made at an angle on each side again, so that when two backbones of like size are tied together and hung, the flaps will open up to allow drying. The drying of fish slabs must be done in the shade, or the sun will dry out the flesh at a rapid rate, causing the flesh to separate from the skin and become mildewed.

Some of the king salmon slabs are salted by immersion in salt solution for 20 to 30 minutes. The solution is prepared by adding salt to a barrel or pan of water. To test for the right salinity, the Yupiaq mix rock salt with water, then put a potato into it. When the potato floats, the solution is right. This was said to have been learned through old-timers from the outside world, but density and bouyancy were no strangers to the Native mind.

When a a family is out at fish camp bringing in and preparing the fish, the mother and older daughter(s) cut the fish while the younger girls ages seven through ten will watch the process. I observed one middle-aged woman cutting fish that her husband had beheaded and gutted. While she was doing this, her thirteen-year-old daughter was watching her mother use the uluaq to cut the fish. After watching her mother cut several fish, she said that she would like to cut fish also. Her mother did not deny her, but immediately gave her a smaller uluaq and looked among the fish until she found a smaller one that was somewhere between five to seven pounds. She gave it to her daughter and proceeded with her task. The young woman set to cutting the fish while her mother would give a glance at her daughter's work every so often and demonstrate by saying, *"Waten piluku."*

The uluaq, or woman's cutting knife, is a traditional tool. The size determines whether it is used for delicate or heavy work. The one for cutting fish is usually five to six inches across its curved blade. For cutting though fish bone, the front end of the blade is placed against the bone; then pressure is applied with the hand and arm. The cutting force can be awesome because the arm, the handle, and the blade become aligned when weight is applied. For filleting, the blade and wrist become a smoothly operating machine. If the cut is away from the woman, the filleting is started with the front of the blade, and the wrist is rotated away as the cut is made. The woman does the opposite move if she is cutting toward herself. Many women have very smooth, efficient wrist movements, bringing their hands back and forth to make deft, even cuts. The uluaq is truly a marvelous tool, using a minimum of materials and energy, and has numerous uses.

The modern fish-cutting table is usually covered with a piece of shag or all-weather carpet. In times past, it was a practice to cut fish on a patch of ground covered with grass. In the upriver areas where spruce trees abound, bark was used to keep the fish from slipping around. The slime from the fish makes any surface slippery, so these means were used to overcome this troublesome problem. After a period of use, the carpet surface has to be washed or scraped with the blade of the uluaq to remove the slime.

Boys eight to fourteen will often go out set netting or drifting with their father or older brother(s). Here again there is a minimum of verbal instruction, with the younger ones expected to watch. The father may say, "This is the right spot to set the net." Upon picking up the net, those with experience will demonstrate how to free the fish from the mesh, how to handle the fish, and estimate how much will be enough for the women to handle. One does not want to exceed the capabilities of the other members of the team. A new practice is having one person pull in the float line while another handles the sink line, and either one or both remove the fish.

Occasionally, the net may hit a snag in the river. Immediate action is taken to start picking up the net, so that it becomes almost perpendicular to the caught end. As much tension as possible will be placed on the net until the boat lists to the weighty side. Once this is accomplished, a foot is placed on the net to secure a hold, and the boat is gently rocked, making sure to take up the slack without breaking the rhythm, until all of a sudden the net will float to the surface. In so doing, the fisherman has used a simple machine, the lever or a modified version of the pulley, and has exerted a minimum of his strength to free the net, using instead principles of weight, energy, and force very effectively.

Fish entrails are used either for dog food or thrown into the river. Different parts of the fish are used or preserved to give variety during the winter. Some fish heads are dried and smoked or salted for winter use, first removing the gills and then splitting the head in half. Some of the fish eggs are hung on horizontal poles to dry. Once dry, a layer of dried eggs is formed in a wooden barrel, followed by a layer of fresh eggs and then another layer of dried. This alternation continues until the top of the barrel is reached; the men make sure that the top layer is dried eggs. They are then covered and placed in the ground or in a cool, dry place. This local caviar serves as high-energy food, especially in cold weather, and will keep indefinitely. Even if it becomes like ash, it will still be edible. It can also be used to make soup in conjunction with edible plants.

Another way of using fish eggs, as told by an elderly woman, is to make a pit, line the bottom and sides with grass, and place the eggs inside. Cover the eggs with grass, then earth. Again, the eggs will keep indefinitely, and even though they may dry up, shrink in size, and become very much like ash, they will still be edible. This woman said that her husband predicts there will be great starvation in the future. Being mindful of this, she has made sure that she has eggs put away where she could find them in case of future need.

Tepa, or stink heads, is a delicacy among the Yupiaq. To prepare it, a shallow hole is dug in the ground, grass is placed in the bottom, and king salmon heads placed on the grass. The salmon heads are then covered with another layer of grass, and earth is piled on top. It is recommended that this be done in loamy soil. Sandy soil will hasten the bacterial action, causing the heads to cure too fast. The closer the fish are to the surface of the ground, the faster the bacterial action. With about a foot of earth over the fish, they will be edible in about two weeks. It is usually the practice to check every so often by digging a small hole to see, feel, and smell readiness. If one wants to have the fish ready in several months, then one digs further down. If one wants to have the fish keep for several years, then it is necessary to dig down to the permafrost. The Yupiaq are very knowledgeable about refrigeration and have used it effectively to preserve fish, berries, meat, and seal oil.

When the fast-tepa are ready, in about two weeks, the required amount is removed, washed in the river, and made ready for consumption. One must be careful not to eat sweet foods, berries, or fruits at the same time, as this will cause a reaction resulting in severe stomachaches. The remaining tepa is kept covered, sometimes curing beyond consumption, in which case it is left in the ground to become part of the soil.

Fresh fish are not to be placed in man-made material containers, such as plastic, as it is likely to induce botulism. The drying and curing of fish is never to be done in direct sunlight, for it will develop a bacterial infection causing sickness or death. Another practice is to cover the fish with grass, cover the grass with a layer of wood, then seal it with a mound of soil. Once this has been done, it is a rule that no fish be added, as this upsets the curing. Fish stored in this manner can be kept indefinitely. When dug up, they can be eaten as is or cooked. The safety practice to keep in mind is to make sure there is no way for flies to get to the fish, for if they do, it spoils and is no longer edible. The people have to be highly aware of temperature and bacterial action and use their senses to gauge edibility. Under proper care and conditions, the end product will be nourishing food.

One of the elders told a story to illustrate the need to store fish carefully. The family was in their camp when their father died. They no longer had a provider, and they ran out of food. The mother remembered a pit filled with fish quite some time ago. It was a very old pit, and she remembered that it was somewhere around the cache. The young boy took on the task of looking for the pit in the cold of winter. He used an ax to hit the ground, doing this for several days. Finally, a day came when he had gone a little further than before. Upon striking the earth with the ax, he produced a faint ringing sound, so he began to chop into the soil. Breaking through, he found grass, under which were white fish, flat and hard.

Returning to the house, he gave them to his mother, who said they were still good to eat. In the many years underground, they had dehydrated but were still nutritious. This knowledge and advance preparation had saved their lives. The elders say this is very much like putting money in the bank, except that this is food for the future.

An important rule when aging whole fish is to make sure the viscera are removed. They are of different texture and composition and tend to spoil more easily. One elder said that he had made a discovery when he tried to put pike and lush (burbot) fish underground. He later found that the lush fish had only the skin left while the pike were still in good condition. Smelts are another that will not keep in this manner. Yupiaq elders engaged in experimentation to learn these facts.

In places where there were a lot of whitefish, they were often split and dried. When sufficiently dry, they would be placed in a sealskin whose openings had all been sewn shut, except for the neck opening. The dried fish would be placed inside, and after the skin poke (pouch) was filled, whitefish oil would be added. The container would then be placed in a cool food shed or cache. The elders say that fish placed in oil never spoils. This is no longer practiced much in the tundra villages because of the modern freezer, but poke fish is still being made along the coast.

The Akiak villagers have found that it is best to smoke dried fish when they are first hung to dry to prevent infection. The first 24 hours are critical in preventing mildew and bacteria from infecting the flesh of the fish. If infection sets in, the fleshy parts of the fish become soft, spoiled, and inedible. After the initial smoking process, however, they do not require close attention. This was explained to the young sons by the father when the boys were supplying the wood.

The Native Diet

Nowadays, berries can be placed in plastic containers and frozen for later use. Salmonberries, cranberries, blackberries, and blueberries are the most numerous on the tundra and therefore favored for picking and storing for winter use. Most often, these are used to make *akutaq*, which is a mixture of shortening, berries, and sugar, though in these modern times mashed potato mix, dried fruit, or commercial berries may be added to make this popular treat. Berries were an important source of vitamin C during the traditional times. The Yupiaq people often wove grass containers filled with berries and placed them into a lake, then weighted down the containers to keep them from surfacing. It is said that the berries, when pulled out in the fall or winter, were almost in the same condition as when placed in the water. Blueberries were the only berries that could not be preserved in this way, for they would break and escape into the water. Another technique was to line the grass baskets with water lily leaves to help keep them waterproof for better preservation.

Mare's tail plants grow in the lakes, and it was the practice of the people to gather these before the snow covered the ice, to be used much like rice, such as in soups and as a side dish. When people were short of food, this plant was often used to make soup with dried fish eggs or food particles gathered from the fish pits from past times. It is still used by some villagers today. These plants will continue to stand when the lake water begins to freeze, so this is the usual time to go out and look for them and scrape them up and put them into containers in a cool place for later use. Sometimes they are gathered in the springtime as well. The plants are said to be tasteless by themselves, thus the need to mix them with something else.

In times of hunger, lichen are used to make soup. Adding a little fish or meat gives a good taste and is very nourishing. Another local plant that is used as a vegetable is marsh marigold, which is eaten with seal oil. The root of the Alaskan cotton grass provides *anlleq*, or mouse food, which the people go out in the fall to retrieve from mouse storage houses. This mouse food was eaten with fish eggs or cooked, diced when done, and mixed into akutaq. The young people would be shown how to use their feet to find where the mouse burrows were located.

When I talked with hunters, they pointed out that commercial bread freezes in cold weather, while the homemade fry bread does not, and that frozen fish, seal oil, "cheese" (fish eggs), poke fish, and akutaq are good in cold weather when the hunter is cold. They say that these will get the "internal furnace" going. It has often been said that the younger generation gets cold easily because of the hot meals, junk foods, and poorly manufactured clothing usually made for a more moderate climate.

The elders interviewed were emphatic in not wanting to glamorize or romanticize our ancestors' lives and ways but wanting rather to tell it as they understood it to be. They pointed out that the people back in the old days were healthy because of their diet. They ate Native foods. They did not add anything to their food, as we do now. Because of their Native foods, they had good, strong flesh that healed very quickly. Several elders spoke on the radio station one morning, encouraging young people to eat as much Native food as possible, saying that this would strengthen the body as well as the mind. In a newspaper article, a medical doctor from the Bethel hospital endorsed the consumption of Native foods and advised against use of non-Native junk foods.

The elders have conceived and visualized the ill effects of attractively packaged and pleasing to the palate and olfactory sense modern foods. They say that these weaken the flesh, which then cannot resist disease. One obvious consequence of the change in diet is missing teeth among the majority of the people, especially the middle-aged generation, who seem to be the most adversely affected. Various news media have brought attention to the diet problem with instructions for the preparation of Native foods published in booklet form and recipes given in a weekly newspaper.

Traditional Medicines and Admonitions

The plants that are utilized vary from one area to another, and many of these plants had medicinal uses in the past. Only the useful plants were given names. The others whose use was unknown or which had no special value other than an ecological one were lumped together under one term: *carangllut* (plants). Today, some plants are regaining popularity for their medicinal value. The ones most often used are wormwood, chamomile, and Labrador tea. We have lost many others because of the modern hospital and pharmaceutical products at our disposal, but there are a few village health aides who have knowledge of some Yupiaq remedies to complement the modern drugs when nothing else works. I heard of many instances where modern medicine failed and traditional medicine worked, and some elders say that is because the natural remedies integrate human expectations and spirituality along with using an herb.

Tart berries are considered to be helpful to the health of the person. They are good for skin conditions and often for stomach problems. The soft willow shoot with its skin removed and chewed will numb and facilitate healing of mouth and gum sores or sore throats.

Qanganaruat (wormwood) is often used for treating heartburn or indigestion. This is done by adding the leaves to your cooking or drinking the juice. The elders referred to this as the Eskimo Tums. It is also used to treat arthritis. The plants are cooked and the hot plants applied directly over the affected area, covered to retain the heat. If the location is in the knees, the patient is required to soak the feet in the solution while it is hot. It is said that after several treatments, there will begin to exude a gel, very much like fish slime, from the affected area. Recovery follows. The elders cited several cases, including one within the last ten years. Apparently this plant has many uses. The mothers pick these plants and tell their children when to pick them, how to preserve them, and how they are to be prepared for use. Several homes in Akiak always had the juice of wormwood available, including the home in which I resided. Another of its uses is for treatment of infected cuts. The wormwood is boiled and allowed to dry and then crumbled up into small pieces in the hands. In the times past, this crumbled wormwood was mixed with seal oil and placed on the wound as it was bandaged. These days, the wormwood particles are mixed with shortening first. After a day or two, the bandage is removed, with pus adhering to the mixture, and the wound heals.

Another treatment of arthritis uses ash from the stove. Ash is placed in a pan of water and boiled and then allowed to cool. The ash precipitates, leaving a clear solution. After it cools, the solution is carefully poured into another container, the ash is removed, and the pan cleaned. The solution is poured back into the original container, and the boiling process repeated. During the second boiling, a precipitate forms at the bottom of the pan. When this happens, the solution is allowed to cool. The cooled solution is poured into another container, and the white, hard precipitate is pried loose and removed. The pan is washed and the solution placed back into it. The process is repeated until no precipitate forms. It is allowed to cool, and the affected joints are soaked in the warm solution. After several treatments, the skin breaks out in what looks like sores much like water blisters. The treatment is continued nevertheless. It is said that this solution will "pull out" whatever is causing the inflammation.

The experimental process leading to the development of a treatment such as this had to occur over a very long period of time before its medicinal value was recognized. This required experimentation, using the rational ability of the human being, establishing a process for refining a natural substance, using very practical means at hand, observing and committing to memory the process of change in the solution, and noting the effects on the human body for determination of its effectiveness. The traditional Yupiaq were well versed in experimental methods and in transmitting the knowledge thus gained from one generation to the next.

One elder told of the things learned in the past.

> Back in those days the old men used to say this: "The poor old ella out here, we the inhabitants are damaging it." They would say the period when it would get very bad had not arrived yet. They'd say in the future its inhabitants would really damage ella by not following traditional practices associated with birth, death, illness, puberty, and other things, consisting of abstaining from certain food and activities, not honoring ella. Thus, they would not honor the land anymore. When they talked about how the earth was going to be damaged, they would say it was going to be damaged if people don't abstain from certain foods and activities. That is the way it is now.

Another elder added:

> *Una taringeqerciu* (understand this). This is what I had heard. They would say that if my first child dies I must abstain from certain activities that are prohibited. I would abstain and not participate in some things. When they stop doing certain activities, they are fasting. And again, if my daughter menstruates for the first time, I was to abstain from certain activities. I was to follow certain laws of nature and the land. And again, if my wife has a miscarriage, that was considered very important. They would say if people stop observing these practices, as people begin ignoring these ways, our environment would be damaged, including the land.

Laws of nature and the land as discovered and established by the Yupiaq people down through the millennia are now being ignored. In our new overpopulated villages and confused state of consciousness, we have come to dishonor and disrespect nature and our way of life. One elder pointed out that we do not follow the instructions of nature and obey the natural laws. We, as a Yupiaq people, are instructed not to go against the laws of nature, at least the ones that have not been forgotten or put away in the remote recesses of the brain. "The laws they had are real from way back in time. They should not be disobeyed."

Healing and Mental Health

Not only were our ancestors concerned with physical health, but with the psychological and mental health of the people as well. One rule of behavior was an admonition against promiscuity—men were told not to fool around with women. To be promiscuous or rape women or have sex without their consent was to bring guilt to our body and soul, for which there was no medicine except to admit to another the trouble. To hold it inside was to become sicker. An elder explained that a shaman might tell the affected one, "It's you who committed this act; speak and reveal your secret. If you want to save yourself, speak. Even though it is shameful, talk about it."

Another area where open expression was encouraged was grieving for the loss of a loved one. A person was told to show the grief and not to hold it in. A certain time for grieving was specified, and it was not to go beyond that time. If one continued to grieve, illness was sure to follow. That is why villages practiced the Feast of the Dead to bring to closure the passage of a loved one to another world. It was believed that the spirits of the departed joined the villagers during the ceremony. The namesakes of the loved ones were clothed and fed, believing that the spirits of the departed were receiving these gifts directly. When the rituals and ceremonies were done, the spirits departed. The spirits were clothed and fed and could then make their journey to the land of the spirits. They were remembered with the names adopted by extended family members or other villagers not related. Those with the same name were greeted and accorded the kinship term of the namesake, whether related or not. Unresolved grief was considered a potential danger to the griever.

An elder in the qasegiq was sitting quietly with his eyes closed. Upon opening his eyes, he related a vision he had just experienced. The vision told of the time that the bones of the Yupiaq would reach the qasegiq skylight. He said that when this happens, the "people will become crazy. They will no longer cry over deaths of loved ones or over others." In the traditional past, it was a sad occasion for someone to die in a village, no matter how far away. They termed this *nunalikut*—the village is saddened, or a place of sadness. This is a practice that only the elders and older people recognize today. The death of another is no longer a time for quiet thought about life and the certainty of death.

Several elders said that the people of today no longer have respect for the property of others. They will steal, break, or harm someone else's property with no remorse. They say that the white man's way is to press charges if it is known who the perpetrator is. This does not correct the problem but merely aggravates the situation. It was also pointed out that children now misbehave and do not listen to parents because they are taught what is called the "bill of rights" in the schools: "You cannot do this to me because I have my rights as a child." This adds to their disenfranchisement and alienation from parents and community, with an attitude toward elders as being old and primitive in their ways. The elders say that the traditional way of teaching young children to not steal and harm someone else's property is a better way, using psychology and spirituality to teach the young right from wrong. It is better to teach by myths, early morning instructions to correct behavior when the young mind is not cluttered with other concerns, and role models, with an emphasis on developing an understanding of the consequences of dishonesty and misbehavior.

It is important to understand the extent to which our Yupiaq ancestors believed in the need to maintain a balance of mind, body, and soul. This is why there were abstinence and fasting rules that accompanied deaths, miscarriages, puberty, menstruation, and so forth. These were made not only to balance one's own life, but to maintain balance with the world.

Today, the Yupiaq have many problems because we have lost that essential balance and have become exiles from our own cultural, natural, and spiritual worlds. When the Yupiaq maintained and sustained a balanced life, it is said that there was very little illness. The elders have obviously made comparisons with respect to physical and psychosocial problems and patterns of disease of the past and those of today. Through comparisons and thoughtful discussions of observations among themselves, the elders have retained the tools for doing investigative thinking and problem solving. The elders corroborate this fact through their lives, myths, legends, and stories.

Technology and Modern Life

The villagers have readily adapted to the use of modern conveniences: propane and oil cook stoves, coffee makers, Coleman stoves, microwave ovens, electric hot plates, refrigerators, and freezers are all found in abundant use in the villages. Everyone watches television without realizing the negative effects of it. It is only now being assessed as being very destructive of some of our cherished values, traditions, and culture (the practice of visiting in particular). No one yet knows how to control the time allotted to television and its impact on the young. It establishes an unattainable wish for the materially based American dream, which is not possible in rural areas, or in the cities for most folk.

Three- and four-wheeler all-terrain vehicles abound in the villages for transportation and carrying packages, oil and gas cans, fish in plastic containers, and wood for the winter. While the imported technology serves many useful purposes, it also presents numerous problems to which people must apply their ingenuity. There was one man who had a trailer for his four-wheeler. One of his big balloon tires had a hole. He checked around the stores and asked friends if they had patching materials. There were none available. After thinking about it for a while, he got a small piece of driftwood, carved it, making one end conical, and made a cut about 1/4 inch into the circumference of the one-inch diameter piece of wood. After forming it thus, he inserted the conical end into the hole and cut off the remaining exposed wood, leaving about 1/2 inch exposed. He proceeded to pump up the tire; and once it was inflated, he was able to go on his errand of gathering wood. He later said that he even improved on his improvised plug.

I ran into another man with a long piece of gnarled wood on the back of his four-wheeler. Since my son and I were using a chain saw, I offered to cut it for him. His response was, "No, I am going to use this for a crosspiece for my fish rack." We asked why he was using this particular piece of wood. He replied by saying, "This piece is very strong. You see the twisted grain? This is what gives it strength compared to trees with a straight grain." We looked at it closely, and sure enough the grain was twisted. I suppose it was due to a combination of wind and snow and ice load during its early growth that caused this. It must have taken many years of experimentation to come to that conclusion.

The sleds of today are entirely different from the carefully constructed sleds of the past. The early sleds were constructed for lightness, flexibility, and ease of handling. This was done by cutting and drying spruce or birch and splitting the dried wood into strips. The strips were planed and shaped, holes were drilled for fitting uprights and for tying, and strong thongs of skin were used for tying joints. The finished product was very light and flexible, but with a good payload capacity.

Today's sleds are made of two-by-eights, two-by-fours, and plywood. These materials are used because of the ease of construction, and the extra power required will be provided by a snow machine, not dogs. They are heavy, but a powerful machine will provide the necessary pulling force. The animal-bone runners of the past have been replaced by fiberglass. Before fiberglass, runners were steel for moderate temperatures, and hard wood for cold weather, with the variations in coefficient of friction accounting for the differences. The elders complain that the sleds today are very noisy along trails, acting much like drums. They can be heard from a great distance as they are pulled over bumps, so they scare the game further away from the trails. Also, the fumes from the machine and occasional leaks of oil and gas cause certain game animals, such as mink, to move away from their natural habitat. One elder proposed using machines only up to a certain distance from animal habitats and either walking or using a dog team to go into the area.

Dog teams seem to be making a comeback in a limited way. With the high cost of fuels, it is not surprising. As one of the elders said, "the dog teams may be slower, but they get you there." Several deaths occur each year because of broken machines or running out of fuel. The users do not take the precaution of carrying survival gear in case of breakdown. The modern Yupiaq have such faith in the power and supposed infallibility of the technological product of the Western world that they do not think of potential dangers to themselves.

Travelers are told to carry some food, an ax, shelter, extra clothing, spare parts, and tools when going over the rivers and tundra. Many people have lost their lives because of the belief that the machine will get you there in a short period of time. The elders point out that the machines do break down, there is always the possibility of a weather change, and accidents may happen. Never take conditions for granted. It is always heartening to hear the elders talk about survival tactics on the news media. Wisdom that has been gained down through the many years is still applicable today.

Yupiaq fish camp facilities have changed, although a few Native people still choose to carry forth the tradition of using a wooden frame for a tent and a smokehouse frame and drying racks made

◀Modern toboggan sled (foreground), traditional basket sled (behind), dog kennels (center).

of driftwood. Most people nowadays have one-room shells of plywood on frames of two-by-fours (no insulation is necessary in the summer), with a wood stove and often a steam house for bathing. A few still have the traditional fish cache on stilts. The pilings on which the structure rests usually have metal covering made from tin cans nailed around the circumference of the piling close to the top to keep rodents from getting into the cache and doing damage to its contents. A few caches in Akiak are placed on 55-gallon drums. The more affluent Native people have small gasoline-powered generators at fish camp to run a TV and other small appliances. There are many non-Native people who have fish camp sites along the river as well. These are usually more elaborate and have the look of the owners who are well-to-do.

Aluminum boats are used extensively. Very few families use the traditional wooden boat. The metal boats are not made with the villager in mind, so some men make modifications to fit their needs. These might include a stern deck made of two by fours and plywood; a control box for the outboard motor gearshift, speed regulators, and steering wheel; and a small housing unit in the aft section to protect the driver from wind and the elements. For those that catch only a limited number of fish for the winter, there may also be a board about twelve inches wide with sidings that extend an inch or less above the surface of the board. This trough is placed over the top edges of the boat and allows the owner to clean the fish in the boat and slide the heads and entrails into the river. Then the rinsing of the fish is only a matter of dipping the fish into the river and washing it off. These people have had to assess what they think was needed, plan, and implement the idea.

The uluaq, or woman's knife, was mentioned earlier. Traditionally, the handles were made of moose horn, bone, wood, or caribou antler. Some families now use wood handles from broken or worn knives because the handles are often of hardwood. Very often the women have to cut fish in inclement weather, so rain gear of all kinds are used.

Large 33-gallon garbage bags are often used for aprons or raincoats. A hole is cut in the middle of the bottom of the bag and two holes cut in the side. It is said that they are very serviceable and do not collect moisture on the inside. Smudge pots using rotting wood, or punk (a fungus growth on trees), ward off mosquitoes in fish-cutting areas.

The school possesses a fishing permit enabling local knowledge-able and skillful men to teach the young boys how to look for locations for setnetting and how to go about drift netting. Girls are taught the process of splitting fish by the women. This is done mostly by example, with little commentary or answering questions from the girls. The little verbal input that is provided consists of telling why certain ways are used for cutting and processing the fish.

Village Life in Changing Times

The Yupiaq people have found many ways to adapt to changing times through a blending of old and new. Sometimes the blend has met with success and other times it has not. For example, most villagers have no qualms about taking advantage of federal and state grants for generating electricity, roads, airports, housing, and assistance to the needy. This has brought new opportunities to the village, and local administrators have learned to account, budget, report on activities, and to live by the rules and regulations attached to these new institutions. From the point of view of some elders, however, this is seen as a disease of the newer generation, especially with respect to assistance to the needy. In their view, it has effectively relieved villagers of their self-esteem, self-reliance, self-sufficiency, and self-determination.

As outside interest and influence in the region grows, possible commercial ventures have been advanced, including tourism, hunting and fishing, guiding, bird watching trips, raft trips, and a whole host of other ideas for bringing income to the area. The village corporation in Akiak has set up a sport fishing recreational project on the Kisaralik River. The villagers want to have control over the number of people allowed into the area—a form of ecotourism in practice. The villagers have realized that too many people and uncontrolled use of the area will bring destruction, but they must also be mindful of the uneasy tension between profit and preservation. They have done the best they can to prepare for the impact of outsiders, knowing that use of this area will disrupt the balance of flora and fauna. They have realized that with a camp and people traveling on the river there will be problems with human and commercial wastes. However, in their planning, including consultants and studies of other projects, they have tried their utmost to strike a balance between the frailties of the ecosystem and the pressures for tourism and sport fishing. At this point, the project is strictly fishing, and therefore the danger of commercializing the Yupiaq culture is not immediate. The village corporation board meetings are open to all villagers, so all are informed of the project and its progress.

An interview with a middle-aged dog musher illustrates how some people have successfully integrated old and new ways on their own. He has 35 dogs in his kennel. He feeds his dogs fish until the fall, then switches to commercial dog food interspersed with fish. He has a brand that has worked the best for him. He has had to develop a knowledge of nutrition, stamina, diseases of the dog, and signs of nonproducers. To do this, he has to have knowledge of each dog individually, its personality, strengths and weaknesses, and conditions under which it performs best. He must be able to diagnose disease, for example, tapeworm, distemper, diarrhea, and so forth. He must be able to remedy these. He has had to work with a veterinarian and read materials on dog diseases and vaccinations. He has been trained to vaccinate dogs and, therefore, does it for other dog-team owners. The traditional use of the dog team has changed drastically from that of pulling heavy loads to one of racing great distances pulling a light sled. The dogs must be sleek and muscular rather than heavy as in past times. He has been adapting to new knowledge and ways with dogs and sleds.

In the Yupiaq region, medical knowledge and practice seems to show the highest level of integration of modern with traditional knowledge. The Native health aide or community practitioner uses the stethoscope, sphygmometer, and visual means of diagnosing and often communicates with the patient in Yupiaq. He or she uses modern means of record keeping, and in cases where symptoms are not understood, consults with a medical doctor over the telephone. He or she is able to dispense pharmaceutical drugs at her or his discretion or on advisement from a doctor. In worst-case scenarios, the aide arranges for medical evacuation to the Bethel hospital.

Most men of the village are in good physical condition because of the type of life they lead. The subsistence way of life requires that they use the mind and the body, very different from the modern person who sits behind the desk and uses a computer to make a living. In most office work, a physical body is relatively useless except for the psychomotor use of hands, so the worker must seek jogging, aerobics, and other means of excercise to keep the body in shape. Keeping in shape is the least of the villager's worries.

The village elders advise respect of the river. The wind, currents, and cold can be lethal. They say that those who use alcohol, drugs, or inhalants such as gasoline and glues lose respect for the river and lose their lives. They say that the river gives life and takes life. Again many tips are given by radio, both in English and Yupiaq. Radio and TV certainly have been forces of integration. Health and survival tips, news, talk shows on sovereignty, subsistence, myths, legends, lifeways, ways of doing things, and messages are often conveyed by these means.

Among the elders, comments about needing enough king and chum salmon for the winter were heard quite often during the summer, while comments about needing enough dollars for the winter were never heard. Younger people, however, who have large aluminum boats and powerful outboard motors are under pressure to make payments during the summer, as there are very few jobs in the winter. The pressure is so great that they have to make as much money as possible to make payments so that their boats and motors will not be repossessed. It is said that those who hold jobs have to be married to the job to be able to make payments. In fact, a number of fishermen are usually caught fishing during closed times or areas. This is unfortunate for Native subsistence hunters and gatherers because they often have to break federal and state laws and regulations to make a living. These are some of the pressures brought by modern financial institutions, often leading to mental strife for the borrower. Some, perhaps, go to the point of excess in seeking resources of value and forget about the balance of nature. Bigger and faster seems to be among the new values that Native people have adopted.

Akiak villagers are concerned with problems of sewage and garbage. These include the many cannibalized machines, such as trucks, cars, three- and four-wheelers, outboard motors, and damaged metal boats that abound in the villages. One home in Akiak has four useless outboard motors, three all-terrain vehicles, an aluminum boat, a wooden boat cut in half, and other metal fragments of items lying around as reminders of our inclination to a throwaway society. Pollution as a problem is just now beginning to be recognized by the village people. They are beginning to see that sewage and materials from packaged goods which they buy account for pollution within the village.

A relative of mine has adopted the practice of cleaning and arranging his yard. Since he has been in the modern world for many years, he has acquired an outside sense of aesthetics. He has cleaned up his yard, planted flowers, and maintains a garden in his front yard and one on his former property as well. He has transplanted

rhubarb, rose hips, ferns, and other wild plants to his front yard. He is the only one in the village who has adopted this practice. He also has about five alders growing in his front yard; however, they tend to grow outward in a disorderly manner. To control this, he has used nylon rope to tie them together so that growth will occur upward, and they will be grouped in a desirable way.

I came upon a young man in his early twenties who was working on a 30-horsepower outboard engine. I asked him if he had gotten formal training in small engine repair. Another man was with him and it turned out that the other person was there to give advice if needed, as he knew about engines. The other man said that this was the first time that he had worked on this particular kind of outboard motor. I asked if he knew how to work on other types of engines and where he got his training. He said that he knew how to make repairs to chain saws, snow machines, and electric generators, and that some of his training came from the National Guard. He said that he learned most by taking engines apart, figuring out the problem, and making the necessary repairs. One time during a training camp, another outfit had generator problems that their mechanic could not repair. They sent for this man, and he found the problem quickly. It was a clogged fuel line. The young man working on the engine commented, "He is a good person to have around when repairing an engine. He knows them well." He is a small engine mechanic of the highest caliber, self-trained in problem solving, who does not even possess a high-school diploma.

Some people seem to place more importance on taking care of the things they own than others do. This is no longer simply a matter of keeping things in repair, however. Since there are now problems of stealing and vandalism, the owner of a boat has to remove tools, gas tanks, oars, and anything else not bolted down and make sure the motor is chained and locked to the boat. There still does exist a vestige of honor and respect for someone else's property, as shown in a story told to me about one of the villagers who forgot to lock her house when she left the village for several weeks. Upon returning to the village, she found that no one had entered her place and that nothing was missing from around the house.

Most items produced by the modern world, such as guns, steel traps, TVs, microwave ovens, refrigerators, and snow machines,

◄Buried under the snow are sections of a wooden boat, two cannibalized outboard motors, a damaged aluminum boat and two four-wheelers.

produce noise. This is a very real difference between Western technology and the nature- and culture-mediated Yupiaq technology. In addition, Yupiaq tools, like an uluaq, which were designed, fashioned, and modernized by the Yupiaq mind, are to be used, not owned. It always surprises me to see houses falling into disrepair, rifles and shotguns rusting, and many other modern tools and appliances lying about, not being cared for, while Native artifacts, such as harpoons, ice picks, adze, and crooked knives, seem to be much better cared for. One elder said that fur hats are "so much more efficient, warming, and closer to the heart" than manufactured hats made of man-made materials. Maybe there is still a oneness with nature and all beings that governs the modern Yupiaq worldview.

Summary

The presentation so far of the Yupiaq applications of science and technology shows that the Yupiaq people survived by learning to ask the right questions, use extensive observation (requiring self-discipline), experiment, memorize useful data, apply data for explanation of natural phenomena, and use available resources to develop their technology. All of this was done in such a way that there was minimal conflict among science, nature, and spirituality. To do so required that certain qualities be present. Empathy was a necessary and desirable trait to give consideration to the needs, rights, and feelings of fellow human beings, nature, and the spiritual realm. Empathy also means that the person has self-control and can abstain from doing what he or she wants in order to do what seems right.

Heterogeneity of experience and perspective is another key to a successful and satisfying life in a rural village. Once a person gets out of the village on the river or into the tundra, the homogenization and standardization brought on by man-made things slowly fades away to the heterogeneity of landscape, flora and fauna, weather, and ever-changing conditions. One becomes a part of the ecological system, as if assuming the "cosmic" consciousness, a sense of oneness, a synchronicity with the universe.

Down through the millennia, the Yupiaq people produced and maintained a science and technology to support a sustainable social and economic system in tune with nature. At the advent of the white society, the Yupiaq ways were pronounced primitive and savage and therefore either to be destroyed or changed to foreign ways of life. Most Native people slowly adopted and adapted in varying degrees to the new ways of being, thinking, acting, and doing. However, the subsistence way of living would not be completely given up. It traditionally has worked for the Yupiaq for thousands of years, so why should it not continue to work today with adjustments to and the melding of the Yupiaq and the technomechanistic worldviews? This is one of the primary reasons that the Yupiit Nation came into being. Several years ago a Yupiaq elder said to me, "the majority of prime land is owned by newcomers, but the few real Yupiaqs are still vigorously Yupiaq. You can educate us, change our dress, change our ways, but we still have black hair, brown eyes, yellow skin, language, and are Yupiaq as hell."

Chapter 4

Education and Science in a Yupiaq School

I chose to study the role of education in the development of scientific understanding, as it is experienced by Yupiaq people in the Kuskokwim region. How do Yupiaq students learn about science in the school, and what implications does that have for the integration of Yupiaq and Western scientific traditions? I addressed my questions in the context of the school in Akiak, where I observed and participated in classes, interviewed teachers, and reviewed the curriculum being used.

Education: The Meeting of Old and New

Western science tends to emphasize compartmentalized knowledge (by disciplines) which is often decontextualized and taught in the detachment of a classroom or laboratory setting (Berger 1977; Franklin 1990; Livingston 1981). Native people, on the other hand, have traditionally acquired their knowledge of the world around them through direct experience in the natural environment, whereby the particulars come to be understood in relation to the whole and the so-called laws are continually tested in the context of everyday survival. For a Native student imbued with a Native experiential/scientific perspective, the typical classroom-based disciplinary approach to the teaching of Western science can present an impediment to learning, to the extent that it focuses on compartments of knowledge without regard to how the compartments relate to one another or to the surrounding universe.

Another potential interference to learning by the Native student is the domineering, manipulative aspect of Western science and technology (Capra 1984; Deloria 1990; Franklin 1990; Milbrath 1989; Page 1989; Rifkin 1980), which is often contradictory to the Natives' view of who they are, what their places in the world are, and how they relate to them. Native people have learned to live in harmony with the earth for millennia by developing a complex integration of cultural values, traditions, spirituality, and an economic base tied to the land. They have not supplanted natural plants and animals and have acknowledged nature's supremacy through its natural forces and processes. They have acknowledged that nature is dynamic and, concomitantly, that people and cultures must be also.

Western thought also differs from Native thought in its notion of competency. In Western terms, competency is based on predetermined ideas of what a person should know in a certain body of knowledge, which is then measured indirectly through various forms of tests (Franklin 1990). Such an approach does not address whether that person is really capable of putting the knowledge into practice. In the traditional Native sense, competency had an unequivocal relationship to survival or extinction. You either had it, or you didn't, and survival was the ultimate indicator.

Western science and technology are more than ways of knowing but also consist of particular practices and methods. According to Ursula Franklin, "The scientific method works best in circumstances in which the system studied can be truly isolated from its general context" (1990:39). This process of isolation is expanded upon by Jim Nollman (1990:74) when he indicates that "the objective viewpoint cannot perceive the context of the whole because the objectivists, themselves, insist upon utilizing only a part of their/our whole being." Nollman goes on to say that this viewpoint places a perpetual buffer between our conscious thoughts and our "very important gut connection to nature." One of the interests of the Western corporate world has been the natural resources found in the Arctic. In their desire to exploit and extract these resources, they have overwhelmed and displaced the people indigenous to the land. From a scientific isolationist perspective, the Native people are considered transmutable physical elements of the environment and objects that can be removed to a new village site, where they often become "human animals in a cultural zoo" (Hall 1988:217). Already, there are several villages where affluent outsiders can fly in to view the Native in the "natural" habitat, a demeaning practice to the people on display.

In the past, Native people tended to view formal education as a hindrance to their traditional ways, but they have begun to look at it in a different light. They are seeking to gain control of their education and give it direction to accomplish the goals they set for it, strengthening their own culture while simultaneously embracing Western science as a second force that can help them maintain themselves with as much self-reliance and self-sufficiency as possible. Having always had to thrive in a tough environment, they know they can make it easier and less harsh, first as humans, secondly as scientists, with a carefully developed technology supported by an attuned educational system.

I have observed and taught in rural and urban classrooms in which science was taught from textbooks, using the scientific method and age-tested science experiments. My own undergraduate science education was derived from textbooks, laboratory manuals, and learning through the scientific method. These teaching and learning processes do not, however, take advantage of the students' environment, or the environment's ecological processes. Nor do they prepare the students to recognize a creative force flowing in and around them at all times. The removal of the mystical force from scientific processes has rendered a society which places primary credence and faith on the rational faculties of human beings, a society which no longer honors and reveres nature, but often misuses, abuses, and disrespects it (Schumacher 1977). Without the ability to integrate the human, natural, and spiritual worlds, science education risks contributing to the decay of the physical environment, with a concomitant diminishment of the resources on which society depends.

A significant difference between Western scientific and Native worldviews is apparent. The Western is formulated to study and analyze objectively learned facts to predict and assert control over the forces of nature, while the Native is oriented toward the synthesis of information gathered from interaction with the natural and spiritual worlds, so as to accommodate and live in harmony with natural principles. Native reciprocity with the natural and spiritual realms implies communication which perhaps must be relearned by the Native, as it is now being learned by Western scientists:

> The science of ecology, the study of the interactions between living things and their environments, circles back to the ancient wisdom found in the rich oral traditions of American Indian stories. Time and again the stories have said that all of the living and nonliving parts of the Earth are one and that people are a part of that wholeness. Today, ecological science agrees. (Caduto & Bruchac 1989)

Education on the Kuskokwim

The school complex is located on the east end of Akiak. The old Bureau of Indian Affairs facility has been upgraded and houses three elementary classrooms. A newer building houses the library, with tables and chairs for class use. A garage for the school vehicle, a school shop well stocked with modern tools, and various other storage buildings are included in the school complex. The newest building is the high school, which has five classrooms, office space, and a multipurpose room that serves as the lunchroom. It is well heated and lighted, and water is pumped to it from the city well. It has most things found in any modern school, including computers, books of all kinds, audiovisual aids, telephones, citizens band radio, facsimile machine, kitchen, showers, and many other items considered essential in schooling.

The Akiak school, headed by a principal, serves sixty-one elementary students, with four teachers, and fourteen high-school students, with five teachers, though responsibilities are shared across the grade levels based on the expertise of the teachers. The school maintains a high attendance and retention rate. However, for the district as a whole, the student achievement scores on standardized tests are among the lowest in the state when compared to overall general scores. The district has implemented several curriculum initiatives in recent years to address this issue.

I was invited by the principal to attend a kindergarten through sixth grade assembly in the library to give recognition to students with perfect attendance (there were four), those who finished all assignments (four), and good citizenship (six). The first group received $2 each, the second a beautifully designed certificate and a can of pop, and the last group received a letter with a certificate and a can of pop. Before the informal presentations began, I was introduced to the certificated teachers, bilingual teachers, teacher aides, and students. It was a very nice get-together, giving students recognition for their accomplishments.

Following the assembly, I was asked by one of the teachers about my interest in science education. He commented that he was taught science from textbooks and that it was such a bore. He learned science the same way in college. He explained that his class had done its first science experiment making chemical models, that the kids enjoyed the project, and that he hoped that they will be doing more before the year was over.

The administrative office houses the various curricula for the teachers. The principal was very cooperative and gave me permission to examine the curriculum guide. Since my focus was on science, I was given the science curriculum guide, which included all grades from kindergarten to high school. I was told that this was the locally developed curriculum presently being used in the Yupiit School District. There were also other science curricula materials available for various grades, but I restricted myself to the examination of the official curriculum currently in use.

The science curriculum guide consisted of a compilation of ideas for lessons and could be easily applied and changed by the teacher. Having seen so many complex and monolithic curricula in my time as a schoolteacher, I found this a very easy document to use. The introduction encouraged teachers to "use the curriculum and adapt to fit educational and cultural needs of students," and to "use textbooks and other materials currently used in classrooms as they work on it."

The elementary curriculum pages were divided into three columns for each grade, with the following headings: (1) concept, (2) learning concept, and (3) activities. This was done for each grade up to grade six, with grades seven and eight combined. The concepts listed for each grade were as follows:

> First grade: senses, living things, earth, staying alive, time, how big, growth and change, magnets, air, rocks, soil
> Second grade: weather and water in the air, sound, light, force, oceans and beaches, parts of plants
> Third grade: living/nonliving things, rocks and fossils, change in matter, earth and solar system, magnetism, habitats
> Fourth grade: earth, light (prism), weather, machines, living things

Fifth grade: ocean frontiers, sound, sensing and moving, electricity and magnetism, living organisms, exploring the universe

Sixth grade: motion and energy, the changing earth, matter and its changes (chemical reaction), human body systems, earth's resources

Seventh and eighth grades: process skills (observing, testing, measuring), living world (chemical symbols and formulas), life processes (diffusion, osmosis, respiration), classifying, development and heredity, ecology, biomes of North America, energy and natural resources

The elementary science teaching is done in two or three 55-minute sessions per week. Except for a husband and wife teaching team who had been involved in some science curricular work previously and who were using materials oriented toward the flora and the fauna of the Alaskan environment, science was taught through the use of traditional commercial science resources and texts. The local Native people were not asked to participate in any of the classroom sessions to share their scientific knowledge.

One elementary teacher was very forthright and stated that he hated science. How did this attitude come about? It was from the way that math and science were taught to him. He remembered math and science as connected to tedium and boredom. In my observations, he appeared to be a bright, concerned teacher, but the teaching of science was on the back burner of his mind. One of the positive things that he had done was to ask the students what they thought might be useful knowledge; he then pursued those paths. The students expressed an interest in the ozone layer based on what they had heard on the news, and so they spent time studying about it. Another session had to do with ecology, especially river erosion. In this, they studied river currents and the way that trees and other plants slow down erosion. This required walking out the door to the riverbank to see the effects of currents and waves caused by winds and power boats. The students were free to draw their observations in bright colors and were encouraged to express their feelings in any way. Another project involved planting seeds and seeing them grow, an enjoyable experience for the students.

Other positive things that this teacher did included developing a scientific vocabulary. He did this by writing down the terms connected with concepts the classes were working on and placing them on the bulletin board. The students were required to write down the meanings in their notebooks. For the development of the terminology and concepts he used available science texts. In addition to these, he used the *National Geographic* to acquaint students with different parts of the world. He had to spend much time explaining, so that students would understand the terms and concepts, though he made little attempt to apply this to the local situation as far as I could see. He did comment that he was thankful for my time, as it got him to thinking about science and about things that the villagers do that might be applicable to science teaching.

Two of the most enthusiastic elementary teachers, the husband and wife, had attended workshops and seminars on teaching science. The two had put together a teaching packet on wolves that had been adopted by the schools in the area. In this, the students learn of the wolf habitat, habits, social organization, and hunting strategies. In addition to teaching, the man was involved in counseling and social work. He had learned to sew skins and showed me the hat he had made for himself.

These two teachers stress making careful observations, making predictions, and trying to figure out why something happened. They use Project Wild, Wildlife for the Future, Model Rocketry, and a standard science textbook. They stress learning appropriate terminology, concepts, and doing some experiments. Just a few weeks before the end of the school year, one of them was doing the model rocketry project. These two teachers certainly were the most enthusiastic about science education. Even though their students received more science and scientific process exposure than the other elementary classes, science was being offered only on Mondays and Wednesdays for 55-minute periods.

The junior and senior high-school humanities teacher, a Yupiaq, did not teach science as such but saw the importance of understanding things about life and knowing what scientists do. He felt that the theory of evolution was crammed down his throat and was taught as fact rather than theory. A Christian, he thought that Christians need to be scientists so that they can support what they believe, and that there is a "lack of a moral basis for science." He believed that teachers of English and science must have a background in technology. He had taken computer courses and taught computer use. He thought the local students are sheltered from the outside world and thus must travel together to other parts of the world to meet other people. He encouraged students to read about other people and used the National Geographic television programs to bring this about. He commented on pollution in the village and wanted the villagers and students to know of it and its effects. He also observed that the Yupiaq family unit was once very strong, but the opposite is true now. He stated that the teachers now have to play the role of parent in some instances. He commented on the fact that he was a junior-high student when Mt. St. Helens erupted, giving him firsthand evidence that nature can change things, and that the students must know of this truth.

The high-school mathematics and science teacher at Akiak had been there for only three years. I found him to be well educated in his chosen field, caring, personable, and of easy-going demeanor, often a requirement in a village situation. But his knowledge about the ways of knowing and skills of the Yupiaq was quite limited. He had the responsibility to teach all math and science in the junior and senior high school. As with most teachers in small rural high schools, he had other responsibilities as well, such as to sponsor a club, to chaperone for school trips to Bethel and other places, and whatever other responsibilities the district superintendent or principal assigned to him. An important impediment to his work was that no science had been taught for five years before his arrival, because no one was qualified to teach science. The students from this period were lacking terminology, concepts, and an understanding of the scientific process.

This teacher's classes were small, only seven students at the most. The classes were well behaved, with cooperative effort by students often displayed and rewarded when a project was successfully accomplished. The reward was a choice of listening to music of the students' choice, playing games involving math, or doing whatever a successful student wanted to do, within reason, on a particular day. The students were very relaxed, listened attentively, and did seat work without being constantly reminded. I never witnessed any disruptive behavior. There was a lot of playful kidding around, joking, and asking of questions, but never anything disruptive.

The teacher established a weekly goal for students to pursue and accomplish. He had one student who was doing advanced work in mathematics and another doing physics. The teacher had a master's degree and a strong background in physics. He taught math and Alaska science to ninth and tenth graders and biology to eleventh and twelfth graders. He had nineteen years' teaching experience, with part of his education at the U.S. Merchant Marine Academy.

In my initial visit with him this teacher stated that I would find science teaching in "the mode of rote." I asked him what science means to him. He stated that science should give the opportunity for the students to practice the skills they have learned and help them begin to use all of their abilities. Science should not be relegated to a discipline; rather it should be holistic. He said that he uses the curriculum, which he thought was devised to meet the state requirements. Most teachers, he stated, are afraid to teach science, especially those that have no, or weak, backgrounds in science. He feels the current science curriculum, which I commented on for its simplicity and brevity, gives him freedom to do things on an individual basis, and that this is important since he has one student in physics and two in second-year algebra.

This teacher stated that the community was only beginning to work with the school, but he feels they have a long way to go. Indications were that local people want more culture taught in the school, but when asked exactly what that means, there was no response. The school needs community direction for cultural development and especially to meet individual needs.

Science equipment was expensive to buy, and therefore this teacher had to try to use everything that was available in the school. He stated that several chemicals were overstocked, and many have never been opened. This, the teacher stated, was due to teachers not having the training or books or manuals to determine what their needs would be.

This teacher cited a problem that I believe is common to all teachers in small rural high schools. The problem is one of balance between academic and practical knowledge, especially for those students who have aspirations of going on to institutions of higher learning. He stated that the academically oriented students needed scientific vocabulary and some basic science concepts. He felt those students needed a classical background in sciences, but he used the Alaska science course as his basic curriculum because it incorporated the environment, developed skills, manipulated experiments, and used the students' abilities. It incorporated other fields such as first aid, safety, earth science, and biology but was weak in botany. The simplified school district curriculum gave him freedom to use new materials and new approaches.

This teacher spent much time on vocabulary and concepts and tried to clarify them through class discussions. He used audiovisual supplements such as "Nova," scientific movies, and other aids. He recognized the Native students' visual acuity and memory for detail. He gave many examples of his students' ability to remember what they saw. Another observation he made was that the students appear uninterested in a lecture, but he had found that they in actuality were listening and thinking.

The students' means of communication with this teacher was to leave notes on their desks for him to read. They expressed their feelings with the subject matter at hand, often pointing out problems that they were having at home, and let him know what they did not understand. Perhaps it was respect for the teacher and the traditional value of holding things inside and acting stoically that prompted this unusual means of communication.

The Native students still respect their elders, this teacher observes. During student body meetings it was often pointed out that elders should not pay admission to attend activities in the school. He felt that communications were hampered because of teacher instability, for every year or two there was a high teacher turnover. The villagers did not want to invest time to teach new teachers the language and culture when they knew that they would likely be leaving before they really learned any of these matters well. If language and culture were to be taught in the school, the Native people needed to teach it or teach the teachers what and how to teach it. Neither option was available. There was even mention that the school was situated on village land and that it should be moved. This man's reaction was to ask "whose school is this anyway?" The sense of the school belonging to the villagers has not been inculcated into their consciousness. There is still the sense of it not belonging to them. The villagers have not formally, through the proper channels, expressed what it is they want Native students to learn.

When I indicated that I was very much interested in the Yupiaq ways of knowing and doing things, the teacher stated that each society has its own way of expressing science. Each society has a way of explaining a phenomenon and is happy with its explanation. I was gratified to hear this from a white man schooled in the Western tradition. He was increasingly aware of the distinctive thought patterns of the villagers.

The physical setting of the math-science classroom was in the northwest corner of the high-school building. In it were desks arranged in rows facing the teacher's desk, along with science books, an aquarium, models of the internal human organs, a poster of the planetary system, an overhead projector, a TV with VCR, and various other science tools. Soft music played in the background. The five biology students, four girls and one boy, entered and settled into their desks. Instructions were written on the blackboard:

"Biology: five pt. bonus on lab test for writing down the differences between plant and animal cells. Three differences, can use the Biology text to research."

I was told by the teacher that the students had spent two weeks learning about the microscope and its applications, followed by a test. He explained to me that life science was offered last year and that this year the teachers were attempting to find ways to use what had been learned during the previous year. This teacher spent time giving instructions as to what to do, what to use, and what to look for. The students were very relaxed, and each went to the corner where the microscopes were stored and returned to the desk with one. There were two boxes of twenty-five slides each of plant and animal cells. After getting a slide, the student placed it on the platform, focused, and drew what he or she saw. There were occasional questions as to which part of the cell was being observed. The teacher went to the student to give help. Each student did several drawings of the various cells. They were to try to see the differences by doing this, then corroborate their findings by use of the textbook. The girls consulted with each other to see what the other had found and to compare drawings and labels. The boy worked by himself.

The math-science teacher indicated that he thought a good understanding and background in math was important. He said that he would be offering chemistry the following year. He expected to introduce the periodic table and possibly concentrate on kitchen chemistry.

Another class session was held, this time with the eleventh and twelfth graders, in the microscope laboratory. There were four girls and two boys. The students rearranged the desks so that groupings of three girls, two girls, and two boys worked together. They got their slides and began making and then labeling their drawings. They showed much enthusiasm for the task at hand. Toward the end of the session, the students began to ask questions not associated with the topic. One boy was interested in vocational education. He asked about the difference in going into academics versus a vocational program. In responding, the teacher stated that the college undergraduate program is probably tougher, as one has to study a broad spectrum of courses.

The student asked how he could get certified to teach vocational education in school. What would it take, and what might be his chances in getting a job upon graduation? He was told that once he got his certification, he would have to earn five credits every five years to renew his certificate. One of the girls entered the conversation, expressing her interest in college. The others acted as though they were not listening, but one could immediately see that they were by the occasional notes written down and a nodding of the head. The teacher had told me that the students would often appear to act indifferent, but they would leave notes on their desks indicating understanding of the topic and would even leave notes asking for clarification. The small class size and the opportunistic approach by the teacher left room for talking about topics of interest to the students.

The five girls and two boys of the ninth- and tenth-grade health class met. An overhead projector was used with a cross-section of the human female reproductive system projected on the screen. The students were to name the components and know their functions. Questions were asked about the various parts and what they do. They were to determine how sperm and egg production occurs and how fertilization occurs. The students were given photocopied worksheets—Human Reproduction: Anatomy of the Female and Male Reproductive Systems and Fertilization and Early Embryonic Development. Two groups formed, one consisting of three girls and the other of two boys and one girl. The interest was keen and the students worked cooperatively. The girls' group worked consistently, but one boy in the other group wandered off and did other things. I was told that he allegedly was a gas sniffer as a young boy, and his attention span had been affected.

The follow-up class was a "Nova" program called "The Miracle of Life." The terms to become familiar with were on the blackboard. There was a class discussion on the terms and what they meant. They were told that the video was the result of microphotography, which was done by incising a small opening in a woman's abdomen and inserting a laparoscope. It was a technological wonder, getting into the small world to see what had been only talked about in the past and seeing it unfold in the Fallopian tube before their eyes. The video was often stopped to review the terms and what was happening in the Fallopian tube.

They learned that there are forty-six chromosomes, which are the genetic molecules that are absolutely necessary for life, that it takes four to five days for sperm to travel five inches, that cilial action moves the egg down the tube, and that there is a twenty-four-hour limit within which the egg must be fertilized. All students listened attentively, but only one, a girl, took notes. They had not been instructed to take notes. During the showing, the students were allowed to arrange themselves in a way that was comfortable to them. Some sat at their desks while others reclined on the floor. The terms and the concepts to be learned were being brought to life. At the conclusion, there was lively discussion about the film. One girl expressed embarrassment at the point in the film that showed a baby's head coming out a vaginal opening. When the students were asked what they thought of the film, the girls giggled. Finally, the slightly rattled girl said, "It was good, except for the ending." This was a part of life in the village as elsewhere in the world and was of intense interest to them.

At the very end of the class, the restless boy went to a cardboard box with light packing material inside. The teacher explained that this was no longer made of plastic but was made of material soluble in water. On hearing this, the boy put one into his mouth, and he opened it to show that in fact it was no longer there. The students were told that this material might be eaten, but they must be careful, not knowing how it had been handled.

Although much time was given to rote learning, the teacher charged the sessions with enthusiasm by allowing the students to ask questions, entering into discussion and allowing them to address topics of interest. The small class size was conducive to this type of teaching. His concluding remark to me was that communication among school, staff, and community was important if changes were to occur, but that it was going to be a long and trying process to change entrenched teaching methodologies to others that fit the village situation.

Native People, Science, and Education

An increasing number of high-school graduates in the villages are idle. Jobs are limited, so these young people create an added burden for housing, recreational facilities, subsistence resources, and other needs. They fit into neither the traditional nor modern worlds, as the schools have not given them tools with which to achieve their aspirations. Their schooling leads to disillusionment and alienation from the Native ways while instilling values and aspirations from another world that is out of reach.

A bilingual teacher aide spoke to me about learning the Yupiaq traditions by having to teach the Yupiaq language. The Yupiaq language holds within it the Yupiaq worldview. The Yupiaq youth are in a confused and disoriented state and should be taught their language, values, traditions, and culture in the classrooms. This would do much to allay the psychosocial problems experienced by the young people. I have heard elders and middle-aged Yupiaq people say that the young people of today "no longer have brains," "have little common sense," and are irresponsible. They are a generation of dependents.

In my discussions with teachers, I often heard comments about the unwillingness of the students to read directions, the discipline problems connected with the students' independent attitude and parents allowing their children to get away with everything. I also heard of student irresponsibility with school property, the sense of ownership due to the sovereignty movement (a movement toward self-governance), and the culture shock they themselves experienced in coming to a place with a different way of being, knowing, thinking, and doing. They acknowledged, however, that discipline has improved in recent years, though students still had a difficult time adjusting to the expectations of the school.

Things have not changed very much since my own elementary, high-school, and college experiences. My own early teaching reflected the same proclivity toward conformity to the way I was taught. Only years later did I begin to try more innovative activities. I think that this had much to do with feelings of insecurity. Everything, including knowledge, the school, the curricula, professional practices, deportment, evaluation, and use of time and space, were handed to me from a preordained world, and it was on these things that I was to be judged and evaluated as a teacher of worth. The teaching methodologies have not changed much, except now there is an overflow of information and, as a result, the content of what to teach becomes problematic (Silvertsen 1990).

Teachers very often feel that they must have control over the classroom, an attitude that can interfere with the kind of learning that can happen when the community, teachers, and students work together. I heard the comment that it was difficult to get the villagers into the classroom. Perhaps the villagers have not been asked into the classroom to speak on things they know intimately. Perhaps the school has not acknowledged and respected Native knowledge and skills. This is one factor that leads me to make the observation that Yupiaq control of education is an illusion. The school board members may be Native people, but they work within parameters established by the state board of education with state rules and regulations. Local control is really in the hands of newcomers, with an administration composed of outsiders.

If the Yupiaq people are to move beyond the illusion of educational control, it will require that the Yupiit School District become Yupiaq controlled, Yupiaq administered, and Yupiaq in practice. Outsiders have to realize that outsiders' control and the resulting forms of curricula and teaching are not well synchronized to Native consciousness. The Yupiaq people have not been dehumanized to the level that they are unable to devise and implement their own programs to release them from the clutches of poverty and self-degradation. The Western models of education and progress have not been able to bring to fruition their promises, so they must acquiesce in their "cognitive imperialism" and allow the Yupiaq people an opportunity to plan and work for their own destiny. Why should someone from the outside come in with foreign values and forms of consciousness and impose them upon another? The people know their reality far better than anyone else.

It is for the Yupiaq people to strive for a school system which recognizes their language and their culture, including their methods of doing science, by which they have learned from their environment and have lived in harmony with it. They do not have to become someone else to become members of the global society but can continue to be their own people. Yupiaq spiritual values are still applicable today because they are nature-based. This Yupiaq consciousness has enabled them to be survivors for many thousands of years up through the 20th century. This survival continues as Yupiaq values, beliefs, practices, and problem-solving strategies are modified and adapted to fit contemporary political, educational, economic, social, and religious institutions. Doing this allows the Yupiaq infrastructure to expand out from the village to encompass institutions such as Native corporations, schools, and churches. The values embedded in these modern institutions are often in conflict with the Yupiaq, so a blending of traditional and modern values becomes necessary.

As Yupiaq people assert greater influence on the educational system, there will begin to emerge a Yupiaq educational philosophy and theories that give cultural and cognitive respect to the Yupiaq learner. Formal schooling can be coupled to the community in such a way that the natural learning that is already taking place can be validated in the same way as the formal learning which occurs in the school. Students can first learn their language, learn about themselves, learn values of their society, and then begin to branch out to the rest of the world. They may later make a choice as to what they want to do and where to live. Given such a foundation, they can fearlessly enter any world of their choice, secure in their identity, their abilities, and with dignity as human beings.

To make the changes indicated requires a teamwork effort between the elders, parents, younger community members, and tribal leaders. The elders have heard statements made that life in these modern days is much easier. They say that this is true only from the material point of view. It is easy to buy nets, traps, refrigerators, microwaves, snow machines, outboard motors, and so forth. It is easy for them to get general assistance and other social service monies to buy their needs. But the elders say that there are hidden costs attached to these material benefits. They are taking part in the exploitation and control of natural resources with a concomitant development of personal avarice and ambition, making them more like the white man. Along with this change is pain and suffering due to conflicts with their fellow Yupiaq people. The money will not flow forever, and what will the Yupiaq people do then, if they lose their language, natural knowledge, and their hunting, trapping, and gathering skills? The elders say they are losing the knowledge and skills needed for survival in a fast changing world.

Recently, the U.S. Congress established a commission to work with Alaska state officials and Native people to "develop recommendations to the Congress and State of Alaska that would help assure that Alaska Natives have life opportunities comparable to other Americans, at the same time respecting their cultures, traditions, and special status" (Blatchford 1990). Having relinquished key aspects of their traditional ways and spirituality in response to an array of physical, political, economic, and educational pressures, Native people have experienced an existential and ontological discontinuity, with extensive social and psychological consequences (Schumacher 1977).

The Western idea of a modern technological world has not been readily accepted by Alaska Native people. Many still opt to live in their own made-from-scratch houses, and they use many of their traditional technological tools in hunting and gathering while adopting a limited number of modern devices. But there are also many others for whom the home environment has changed so much that there is little to remind them of their Nativeness. They all retain one thing in common, however, and that is reliance on a subsistence lifestyle that transcends their physical living conditions and technological conveniences. Although non-Native people tend to view the subsistence way of life as being very simple, the Native practitioner sees it as highly complex. A subsistence-oriented worldview treats knowledge of the environment and each part's interdependence with all other parts as a matter of survival and, as such, provides a complex model for maintaining and sustaining a balance with nature.

Traditional Native subsistence technology was based on the use of natural materials for making tools. These consisted of skin, bone, stone, and wood. This was a nature-based, nature-mediated technology. The technology included metallurgy; naturally refined copper was often used for making tools. The tool-making process was integrated into daily life and allowed sufficient free time for contemplation of natural and mythical forces. Marshall Sahlins has referred to hunting and gathering people as the "original affluent society" (1972:1). His research indicated that these people traditionally spent less than forty hours per week foraging for food. Unfortunately, for many Alaska Native people, this affluence is no longer a feature of their lifestyle.

Native people are beginning to realize that technological and bureaucratic solutions as a road to progress are a myth. Labor-saving tools and consumer-oriented gadgets tend to create a dependency on external resources and expertise that can lead people down a pathway of cultural dislocation and destruction. There is a need to demystify and humanize science and technology, and the place where this can begin is in the teaching of science in school.

Science teaching need not come from the textbooks alone; nor need it espouse the scientific method as the only way to construct knowledge. Rather, what traditionally is understood through myths, collective thinking, experiential learning, intuition, and the ontological presence of mind needed to guide, temper, and get things right should also be included. Ontological discontinuity need not persist. The Native ways, rituals, and sense of sacredness can be understood as outward expressions of a highly developed ecological mind set. According to Gregory Cajete (1986), Native ways represent an ecological mindset of sacredness, with ecological relationships and a constant "seeking of life."

Students can be taught to become thinkers, inventors, and creators, always mindful of environmental balances. Their awareness of Native and Western science perspectives for visualizing a world where harmony exists and where there are comfort and security for everyone could go far to instill the motivation necessary for a better world. Native students' aversion to academic mathematics and sciences is often attributable to an alien school culture, rather than to any lack of innate intelligence, ingenuity, or problem-solving skills. The curricula, teaching methodologies, and often the teacher training are based on a worldview that does not always recognize the Native notion of an interdependent universe. Sioux Chief Luther Standing Bear has said, "The old Lakota knew that man's heart away from nature becomes hard; he knew that lack of respect for growing living things soon led to lack of respect for humans too" (Nollman 1990:3).

Chapter 5

Yupiaq Cultural Adaptation in the Contemporary World

As I survey the uses and effects of modern technology in Yupiaq villages, I see a confused people and a disparity in the distribution of resources, wealth, and goods. Although the Yupiaq have ancient tenure on this land and although they may be sitting on wanted natural resources, they are invariably shunted aside and receive peripheral tidbits from the wealth derived from their land. Contrary to what many people say about an easier life with access to Western goods and services, life continues to be hard and sometimes bleak in the villages. The outside perception of villages as quaint places where people live a romanticized lifestyle persists because we are unwilling to admit that many of our villages are little more than ghettoes by conventional Western standards.

New technological tools and devices are introduced to the villages daily, and although they may seem to make things easier, many of these machines have hidden costs to us and our environment. Take, for instance, the snow machine—a fast, untiring machine with ample pulling power to do the work. But do we consider what the noise does to us and to the game, what the occasional oil leaks and small gas spills do to the fragile tundra, how the breakdowns lead to accidental deaths, and the unsightly cluttering of discarded machines? The snow machine has changed our ways of courting and dating, hunting and trapping, and it makes a big demand on money resources for gas, oil, repairs, and maintenance. These machines were made for the affluent middle class and thrill-seeking Americans. The process of development paid little regard to material costs, mechanical and fuel efficiency, or the degree of technical complexity—in fact, the more complex the better. The Western scientific method is utilitarian and is not disposed to ecological considerations.

We Alaska Natives have lived through the millennia in harmony with our world. It is time that we demand to consider technology before it is introduced to our villages. It is time that we demand of our schools and institutions of higher learning that they make accessible to our Native students an understanding of mathematics and sciences. We need Native scientists and technologists who are capable of looking at development and research projects from two different perspectives, and more importantly, are able to work with elders to develop soft technology in tune with and conducive to nature (Hopkins, Arundale, & Slaughter 1990). Machines are here to stay, but we must find ways to humanize technology with tools that are not violent or destructive to people and their environment.

Soft Technology: Adaptations to Culture and Environment

Traditionally, Alaska Native people developed a nature-based and nature-mediated science and technology to suit their needs, along with the needs of their environment and nature. As Natives have learned to utilize Western scientific and technological processes, it has been with an inclination toward "soft technology" (Lovins 1977), which provides a means to temper Western technology and use it as a tool for adaptation to local culture and ecology. The focus of soft technology can be to upgrade and update traditional skills, to develop tools that can be easily repaired, to be conservational and nonpolluting in the use of renewable resources for energy and raw materials, and to fine-tune the subsistence lifestyle. In searching for examples of implementing soft technology, Paul Harrison has offered the following as representative criteria for its use (1983):

1. improving an existing traditional technique
2. modifying a modern machine

3. inventing a new machine from scratch
4. finding a useful and economical Western antique
5. applying a bit of indigenous wisdom to the solution of a new problem

Traditionally, everything that was used was recyclable and biodegradable. Now, the Native people are wallowing in garbage and sewage. Pollution is an "inevitable consequence of life at work," but now, "there is only one pollution . . . people" (Lovelock 1987:27) and their desire to buy prepackaged foods and gadgets. The educational and economic systems have taught Native people to be consumers, often in the form of inappropriate products, including housing and complex technological tools and machines ill suited to the Arctic. The harsh environment makes many of these externally designed and overly sophisticated products last a relatively short period of time, though their frozen remains last forever. For instance, snow machines will operate an average of three winters and then deteriorate very rapidly. This places an added burden on the owner for maintenance, oil and gas, and replacement. With all these cumulative environmental problems, Native views about the quality of life need to be reassessed in modern times.

Native people are no exception when it comes to modern wants and needs. The numerous TV stations beamed to the villages by satellite present pseudorealities for both young and old. They live torn between the desire to retain their traditional hunting and trapping practices and the desire to obtain the modern advantages gained through exploitation of natural resources. However ambivalent Native people might be, "most people who are on the receiving end of offshore and Arctic oil operations have greeted these enterprises with a comprehensive lack of enthusiasm, because they directly perceive the prohibitive social and environmental costs" (Lovins 1977:4). Indeed, the syncopating lights of growth and development from the Western perspective can be mesmerizing, but Native people have come to realize that they are dealing with a perception of progress that is no longer appropriate for indigenous survival. There are many ecological niches on earth where primal human beings learned to live as a part of their surroundings. But with the onslaught of Western society and the accompanying technology, people's numbers decreased drastically, their identity flagged, and they became dependent on institutionalized social services to make a living.

We have been slow to realize that when we become dependent on outside technology and services, we reduce our self-reliance, self-sufficiency, and identity (Anderson 1991). Let me use a simple example of the Alaska State Housing Authority (ASHA) housing and other government-built facilities in the villages. The architects and engineers may have used the geodesic design and found ways to keep from having to elevate the houses off the ground. Some of this might be good design in the Louisiana bayou, but why was it transplanted to the Alaska tundra? Would it not have been just as easy to ask the local people, "What kind of home, materials, design, and use would you suggest?" Such an approach may have produced a house more suited to the environment, or even fitted to the environment. But we accept without question, because the builders and designers are of the great omniscient and omnipotent society. In our haste to please, we completely disregard our own housing technology, viewing it as being archaic, damp, dismal, and uncomfortable. We forget that it enabled our ancestors to survive for thousands of years: it was heat efficient in the winter, naturally air-conditioned in the summer, circular in form for better air circulation, semisubterranean to make use of the insulative crust of the earth, the framework covered with sod with the vegetation on the inside to make an air barrier, and it was made with available local materials. By accepting the modern house, we denigrate our identity and we relegate a lot of time and energy to the maintenance, heating, and electricity of modern houses. A larger portion of our income from hunting, trapping, fishing, and jobs goes to these new survival items. Why can't we say, "Just wait a minute—before you bring in your version of a new house or school, let us examine the specifications. We don't want another technological dinosaur introduced to our community"?

The economic problems of the Yupiaq are still greater than these. We have no real economic base other than fishing, trapping, and government-funded jobs and services. Finding—or creating—jobs is a difficult task which, if undertaken, must involve Native people to draw up plans and establish goals for their particular region, much as the Yupiaq are doing with the Yupiit Nation. Wage labor is limited, and isolated cottage industries have been tried without success. Perhaps we can draw an analogy from the Amish, who though in constant clash with the American technological society have been surprisingly able to endure. The reasons for their success seem to be that they have a language, have a tie to the land, have a history, have allowed a limited number of technological tools into their society, and train their people for work to maintain their economic system.

From my perspective, it seems that each region needs to determine whether it is going to maintain a quasitraditional lifestyle with only a few basic, culled-out Native values to mix with chosen outside values. This, of course, presupposes that the Native people exercise self-determination and take on the responsibility to work for solutions to their own problems. I would propose that Native people address themselves to local flora, wildlife, and fish habitats and learn to increase productivity without resorting to recombinant DNA, hormones, antibiotics, special feeds, and other artificial means to which Western society is inclined. Native people have always been curious about all living things on the earth and how they interrelate. They have much experiential knowledge gained through keen and patient observation with nothing left to chance. The subsistence lifestyle leaves little room for gambling.

The bogs and marshlands provide an abundant source of nutrients for many species of birds, fishes, and animals. The streams, creeks, rivers, and sea are being rapidly polluted by effluent wastes, erosion, and man's activities. Trained Native people are needed to protect them from further destruction. This may mean, for example, that we compromise our high-powered motors for less speedy, energy-efficient engines, cutting down on pollution and wave action. The boats may become smaller and lighter but with a payload comparable to that of the traditional qayaq. The qayaq may get motorized with a lightweight solar-powered engine. The hunting weapons might be a combination of the principles of the bow, the scuba diver's spear gun, and the rifle. A rifle might be designed with a shell containing an inflatable float and high-tensile line to keep the hunter from losing a seal or walrus. As the shell hits flesh, the float is automatically released. This would minimize losses due to sinking. Thus hunting implements become more humane and efficient. For continuity of lifestyle, experts cognizant of both the traditional and modern knowledge and skills could be encouraged to work in nurturing and enhancing biota and related ecological processes.

Since our traditional ontology places a barrier to "owning" living beings that often possess more power than we, we have to seek new approaches to working with our cousins in the animal world. Our Earth is the giver of life, and we are placed on her to work with her. This is traditionally what we have done. It means a need for a combination of Native experts and cooperating land and wildlife managers, fisheries biologists, hydrologists, architects, doctors, engineers, ecologists, botanists, economists, and chemists, to name a few. We need scientists who are in contact with Native life. For example, the health care services under the village health aide program are closing in on integrating traditional medical practices into the health care system. Psychology and psychiatry remain Western in orientation, treating part of the person without regard to the total being. Elders have much to contribute through their lives, their mythology, and their ceremonies in establishing balance in the whole of life. After all, the Spirit of the Universe gave us the ability for rational, intuitive, and mystic communications so that we may know what to do to work in balance.

Why then are we so troubled? I can advance one possible explanation. We, as Natives, are blinded by Western knowledge and its technological products, often confusing means with ends. The syncopating strobe lights have been transformed into a myth, a religious play, and we faithfully accept these gods of the new world. It is now time for the natural, the primal person to step in. We have remained quiet but must now begin to pose questions to young people on the appropriateness of the modern, utilitarian scientific method and its products. This is a demythologizing task, calling into question science for science's sake, technology for technology's sake.

Many of communications, medical, and transportation techologies, like various appliances, have been very useful to Native people, but for many superfluous gadgets, we pay dearly by surrendering our self-reliance, our self-sufficiency, and our identity. We confuse our children, whom we recognize as our greatest resource to carry and transmit our culture and values. We voice and espouse the value of our ways but eschew our traditional and technical tools and methods in everyday life. We leave to the formal school setting the teaching of language, values, and techniques by employing Natives through "supplemental" programs, such as federal Indian Education and Johnson-O'Malley Act funding. I am not saying that it is bad for the school to be involved in cultural transmission, but is it a true extension and reflection of the home and community? We are no longer traditional Alaska Natives. Men are no longer full-time hunters. Women are no longer full-time homemakers. Our youngsters are confused because our cultural template has been unrecognizably eroded.

The task is to carefully reconstruct and redefine ourselves by replacing missing pieces to engender a new Native identity, its infrastructure built around valued Native traditions. Right now it is emotionally and mentally costly to try to succeed in either world, much like trying to fit a round peg into a square or triangular hole. So our youngsters enter school confused and graduate confused and disoriented. They may show signs of pride and smugness for being Native, but, I venture, it is often a fragile facade. Anxiety is ready to burst as an antisocial act at any questioning or slight of this supposed Native reality and being. Is it any wonder when we complain about owning substandard ASHA or HUD out-of-context housing, relying on the store for a hard-to-fix four-wheeler, shopping at Sears-Roebuck for myriad specialized appliances, paying the grocery store for less-than-nutritional food, or receiving the late general assistance check? We are trying to become what we are not meant to be—a dependent, specialized, and homogenized people. We have become, as the *Anchorage Daily News* (1988) put it, "A People in Peril," a consequence of confusion and disillusionment. Therefore, I propose synthesizing the traditional with modern technologies to create a soft technology, reflecting a people at home in their own dynamic and technology-enhanced environment, working as philosophical tenders of the earth.

In the past, Native people tended to view formal education as a hindrance to their traditional ways, but now they must look at it in a different light. We must control education and give it direction to accomplish the goals we set for it, strengthening our own culture while simultaneously embracing Western science as a second force that can help us maintain ourselves with as much self-reliance and self-sufficiency as possible. We must learn to thrive in a tough environment, and we can make it easier and less harsh, first as humans, secondly as scientists, with a carefully developed technology. Soft technology is intended to help people become the producers of those things that are needed for human support and comfort.

Alaska Natives and Schooling

In reviewing the previous descriptions of the contrasting worldviews that coexist in Yupiaq communities, one begins to see that various characteristics can clash with one another (Chrisjohn, Towson, & Peters 1988). For example, the holistic approach to teaching and learning of the Native people represents a significant difference in perspective from the incremental and componential ways of Western education. The modern idea of progress results in circumstances where "the mindless rush for new tools, discoveries, and physical progress proceeds at an ever accelerating rate; now the earth itself sheds tears of abuse and environmental stress" (Simonelli 1991:58). Superficially, there appears to be no relationship between modernity and traditional Native ways of life. However, ways have to be found to integrate some ways of modernity into a new Native consciousness or "being in the world" (van Manen 1990:11). Much modern ideology needs redefinition to fit a new consciousness that can lead to a new form of education for being and becoming. Among the areas for expansion are curricula, policies, language of instruction, teaching methodologies, educational philosophy, administrative practices, educational goals, and their related objectives.

The person charged with the responsibility for administration and coordination of all activities in the rural schools is the principal. Since the inception of schools in rural Alaska, this figure has been the primary agent of Western ideology (Berger, Berger, & Kellner 1974:103). The pool of Native administrators is limited by the educational system to a handful, so that villages, through their advisory school boards, must carefully interview and select their principals from a pool of external applicants. In this situation, the attitude (such as a positive attitude toward the people with whom that person will work) of the principal is critical to the success of the school system. Boards should consider whether that employee is willing to work with less-educated people and take risks in innovative and nontraditional methodologies and programs different from what that person has experienced before (Hardwick 1991).

The principal must also be willing to accommodate the complex and dynamic quality of evolving educational programs and must be team- and people-oriented (Fienup-Riordan 1990; Ryan 1989). In addition, the principal must be adaptive, innovative, and flexible; must maintain a loosely structured administrative approach and possess a high tolerance for ambiguity (Barnhardt 1977). Most importantly, the principal must be willing to talk to people, especially the elders, to become knowledgeable of their thinking and ways of doing things, to become generous in thought and action, to reflect the will of the people, to render actions influenced by the people, to speak out wisely, and to have peaceful and exemplary behavior (Fienup-Riordan 1990; Hardwick 1991). Further, the person hired to be principal must embody the proclivity to consensus, that is, the ability "to arrive at one mind" (Fienup-Riordan 1990:214).

These are the attributes the principal as leader in a village school must possess. Sheilah Hardwick (1991) goes on to say that a leader is like a tree with roots composed of integrity, ethics, and values. She continues by indicating that a leader with this foundation will make decisions based not only on intellect and logic, but on what feels right in the heart. A leader not only has the function of teacher but has an open mind and is therefore teachable. The leader strives for knowledge production from the villagers, with the realization that a broader and deeper knowledge base must be generated. The collective will can wield such potential power, drawing on "a viewpoint or attitude about life which causes such power to be used in concert with a deeper understanding of what it is to be alive" (Simonelli 1991).

With respect to teachers, their selection must be just as stringent as the selection of the principal. Teachers must be willing to learn at least the rudiments of the Native language and culture in order to do an effective job of teaching, for "belief systems are the framework upon which cultures and societies function," and the language is its carrier (Locust, 1988:328). Non-Native teachers may be opposed to this idea, but it is a desideratum if a new consciousness is to be developed. It is a requirement consistent with the Native peoples' holistic teaching and learning.

The principal, teachers, parents, older student representatives, and community members must collaborate in teaching (Scollon & Scollon 1979). This is a requirement if new, innovative and out-of-the-ordinary programs are going to be tried. Close coordination and consultation among the various people within and outside the school system are necessary to produce appropriate information-gathering tasks for school students. Parents and students of different grade levels have to be given assignments to match the students' knowledge and skills. This effort creates a team of teachers, parents, their offspring, and the community. More importantly, this collaborative teaching and learning avoids making obvious the Native students' deficiencies or inadequacies, which the modern system does so successfully (Ryan 1989). Self-esteem and self-confidence will rise as the students deal with things that they know about and that are a part of their life. When they can learn about others through their own worldview, learning and tedium are no longer synonymous. Not only will students' attitudes improve, but the family will come closer together and improve their interpersonal relationships. This is a multidisciplinary, multisensory, holistic, and potentially exciting approach to education—schoolwork connected to the work and play of the community.

Yupiaq Ethnoscience: Implications for Village Education

I have tried to explore the Yupiaq worldview and ways of knowing to form the foundation for a synergistic approach to teaching. As we look briefly at both the Native and Western ways of knowing, we see that there is a scientific approach to both, although one goes heavily into a mystical, pragmatic, inductive way of sense making while the other has chosen a secular, experimental, deductive way. Yupiaq science gets its profound discoveries from interacting with the mystical, transcending the intellectual ability to analyze and understand the world through mathematics and the sciences. This expresses the dichotomy between the two views. They may have started from the same drive to understand and live in the world we were given, but each chose its own way quite removed from the other.

I propose that it is possible to teach Native youth mathematics and, more particularly, the natural and physical sciences by capitalizing on the Native knowledge already existing in their culture. The natural sciences are nothing more than the observation, interpretation, and understanding of the interplay in nature. The Native has perspicacious knowledge of nature. The teachers must realize that the Native students entering school are not empty computer disks or sponges to be filled with facts and knowledge by the teacher. They enter school with language skills already in their minds and the beginnings of an understanding of how they interact and are part of a family. They have the basic qualifications for success required of any student in the world who wishes to become a successful hunter, banker, scientist, teacher, leader, or renowned thinker. Their culture provides a basis to progress in acquiring new knowledge, new skills, and new ideas on how to increase the quality of life without having to dominate the earth and destroy it at the same time, and without relinquishing those values that are deemed necessary to give life and distinctiveness to the group.

I propose teaching mathematics and the sciences through oral literature, mystical philosophy, conservation (including the sacredness of the Native relationship to the land), and utilizing the Natives' special ability in spatial relationships. This can be done with an elder who is a Native speaker and knows the little secrets and idiosyncrasies of the language and can explain a concept in Native terms. Then take the same idea or tool and introduce students to it from the Western perspective, helping them understand the differences. The Western thinker has chosen mathematics and scientific terms and nomenclature to explain the same phenomenon. These questions of semantics take on an exceptional importance, because the Western perspective can lead to further alienation from the natural world, and the learning can become based on words rather than on participation and interaction with nature.

I advance this idea of ethnoscience as a way of improving the teaching of mathematics and sciences, especially to rural Native students, recognizing that youth of the dominant society experience the same difficulties in understanding abstractions and vernacular peculiar to the disciplines. To forget that a child has sight and therefore sees images, has a mind and therefore can imagine, and most often has the ability to draw or doodle is a gross oversight of educators. To make the basic concepts understood in the elementary grades, one has to use all the sensory tools, including visual thinking, and apply them to experiences with which the student can readily identify. However, different values, concepts, perspectives, and philosophy determine how they interpret the empirical data and relate them to the natural world. Each culture, through the millennia, has established a way to make the natural world accessible to reasoned inquiry—exploring what is real, what is truth, and what is good and beautiful. This flows and is channeled through their science, art, and religion. Natural phenomena in the Yupiaq world are explained in terms of readily observable characteristics or experiences involving a high degree of intuitive thought.

This analysis attempts to set the stage for a more systematic approach to teaching, based on a Yupiaq cultural perspective and criteria drawn directly from cultural experience. We will increase the student's understanding and achievement if we provide experiences that build, consciously or unconsciously, on Yupiaq cultural thinking processes. Ethnoscience is nothing more than Yupiaqized or humanized science. There are no good reasons that we are bereft of scientists in our region when the educational system has been in place for more than a hundred years. It just manifests the failing of the educational system to recognize that culture is science and that the teaching methodologies we use are too Westernized in philosophy and thus are biased to that perspective only (Hobson 1992; Pickering 1992).

Yupiaq people have a unified worldview, with a deep appreciation of collaborative teaching and holistic thinking, but the thinking, at least in education, stops there and confusion is rampant. Should the school be bilingual? Which language should dominate? Are we willing to say, "Yupiaq is going to be the working language in our region, with English as the second language"? Educators purport to endorse bilingualism and biculturalism, but their way of thinking often accommodates neither. Our children are on the losing end because of this confusion and may therefore learn neither language, with a resultant Yupiaq cultural gap. As one elder pointed out to me, "My high-school children come home to our one-room house. They are here, but a partition exists between us. They are losing our language and way of life, yet there really is no alternative lifestyle other than subsistence for many years to come. They now have needs and wants based on the white man's way." What a dilemma for a parent to be in.

My personal approach to science teaching, which some will say is idealistic, is that we should make use of the Yupiaq language because it is a tool of the spirit and therefore the voice of the culture. I would pay particular attention to Yupiaq learning style and to the people's application of science principles. Our Yupiaq have been in touch with Nature since the beginning of time. They have been in touch with the Ellam Yua and thus in touch with science, for science is nothing more than curiosity and the observation of how and why things work and how life can be made better through understanding. Since science is basically observation, modern tools only refine our ability to observe, and the written language helps us to record the data.

Elder participation is critical to Yupiaq science teaching. Their thinking, learning, and desire to convey the age-old products of wisdom, including individual and group fortitude, values of life, liberty, and the pursuit of happiness, are based firmly on Yupiaq spirituality and worldview. The premise in teaching Yupiaq science is to begin with the environment, ensuring cultural sensitivity and relevancy, because it is something elders are most intimately in tune with.

I'll use a simple example of an activity exploring science in the fish camp. The science of making tepa leads to the concept of aging by bacterial action, chemical equations, toxicity, and so on. It can be pointed out in this and other activities that the interest of the Yupiaq is the whole product, whereas the Western scientist is interested in breaking down the whole into components to understand the end product and how it got to be that way (in this case without poisoning the consumer).

You can study the splitting of fish using a simple machine, the wedge. Why and how is it done? What are the energy transformations involved in cutting, drying, smoking, and storing the fish? Along with the fish, you can examine the Yupiaq identification of plants and animals, the life cycles, the food webs, climate and weather conditions, the traditional way of telling time, animal behavior and habitats, the common-sense measurements, plant and berry use, refrigeration techniques, inertia in a canoe and qayaq, and many other science principles.

The students will learn to expand their knowledge and skills and would ultimately realize that not only we, but all people of the world, are ecological dependents, and what we do with the environment affects our lives as a whole species. As they progress they would begin to think, "What can I do to contribute to the economic self-sufficiency of my region and make it better environmentally?"

The students would also be expected to master the content areas and do good work in note taking, writing, diagramming, and labeling. Their study should include visual thinking sessions to whet their imaginations so that they see everyday pieces of their environment a little differently. Each exercise would involve thinking in the humanities, as well as math and science. In other words, this should be a multidisciplinary teaching and learning adventure. It can be fun to learn science tied to the world around us and through our own experiences and then branch out to discover universal laws of nature! This is the meaning of Yupiaq ethnoscience—a Yupiaq way of knowing.

Integrating Schooling and Yupiaq Ways of Knowing

The curricula, methodologies, and, often, non-Native teachers and their training are not based on a worldview that recognizes each of us as necessary and interdependent pieces of the universe. Scientific knowledge and teaching is fragmented knowledge that is discriminatory, piecemeal, and analytical. For Native people who have learned from particulars leading to the whole, this can be an impediment to learning, as it addresses a specialized segment of a phenomenon without regard to how it relates to the rest of the universe. The Native student enters school with linguistic skills already developed, having all the qualifiers for success and the intellectual tools of the culture at his or her command. Why then can we not expect to have many scientists from our people?

Science, with its fractionalized detachment, has become anathema to the Native's view of who we are, what our place in the world is, and how we relate to it. Scientific principles are used to develop modern technology; yet one can't help but hear reports, read accounts, and experience the good and the bad effects and therefore ask "just what purpose is science and technology if it is slowly destroying our world?" We have lived in harmony with earth for millennia by developing a complex set of cultural values, traditions, religion, and economic base. This is no easy task. We have only domesticated the dog, have not supplanted natural plants and animals, and have acknowledged our Creator's supremacy through attention to natural forces and processes. We have acknowledged that nature is dynamic, and concomitantly, our people and culture must be also.

The teachers in their education must learn to appreciate the multiplicity of realities that the language, whether indigenous or a version of English, is intimately fashioned to express. It represents reality as the people who use it see reality. Just because our language is different does not in any way make it less real. We Yupiaq, as well as people in the Western world, are beginning to question the world that we have created by scientific technology and its effect on the quality of life. Has it truly made life better? If not, then all the disciplines should address how to make it better, especially in the area of schooling. We are going to have to step outside, take a look at our situation, and formulate a goal that we can implement, at least on a limited scale, as all the world is not ready for a global change. We will have to think less in terms of the artificial level of the quality of life we lead and try to recover the natural processes that are the real basis for productivity. This then brings me to the main purpose of this study, that is, to find a way to integrate the humanities with the sciences and Native knowledge and skills with modern science and technology. Can this be done? What effect will it have on existing curricula?

We Yupiaq know something about Western philosophy and the accompanying educational paradigm, but we know very little about our own because we no longer hear our elders tell the myths, legends, and historical stories that really demonstrate our philosophy. The educational paradigm we have experienced over the last hundred years must not be dispensed with but must be made to serve as one of the foundation stones upon which a teacher-student-community collaborative approach can be developed to address the needs of a fast-changing society. One must recognize that the present society is looking askance at a world wrought askew by science and technology without regard to the life-giving planet Earth. Now our educational system must reassess and redirect itself to a more holistic mind set, which means education must be multi-disciplinary, multidirectional, and multisensory, with the total environment as the laboratory.

The Fish Camp as Classroom

Having identified some of the critical features of a Yupiaq worldview, I will now show the implications this may have for the actual planning and implementation of an educational program, which I will call a fish camp science odyssey. I want to stress again

A Yupiaq fish camp. Fish rack protected by a plastic tarp.

that the so-called bicultural programs in schools go heavily into the material and how-to, or technical, aspects of the cultural spectrum. It is easy even for our people, and especially outside teachers, to emphasize these superficial aspects of the culture. These, after all, are easily understood and do not require any particular analytical thought, merely the appropriate materials and the instructions of an often low-paid Native resource person. Even the storytelling, when taken out of its natural context, becomes more an entertainment tool than an important means of cultural transmission.

I chose the fish camp for selfish reasons. I remember it as being a place of happiness, warm weather, and a place for orderly Yupiaq industry. Also, it presents a cornucopia of traditional and modern technologies. Although we did not have technical names for many natural processes, we used natural, scientific principles in preparing our food; catching fish; reading river currents and tides; assessing weather and wind conditions; preserving plants and edible berries; making plant, fish, and animal classifications; and using solar energy. I propose to use traditional scientific concepts that the student already knows as a basis for exploring new realms. English and Yupiaq will be used interchangeably, with participation by elders a must. The students will be expected to master content, do daily work in note taking, produce writing that includes scientific vernacular, make drawings (technical and artistic), and engage in labeling, speaking, and discussing ways for possible application of an admixture of traditional and scientific principles. Students will be expected to sponsor an ethnoscience fair to culminate the experience.

Much time will be expended for introspection and self-awareness, especially students' feelings toward themselves as a person of worth, their place in the world, and self-aspirations. The ways to do this will include meditation (which clears and concentrates the mind), imagination (the mind's wanderings), and visualization (which puts a spark of life and imagery into imagination). Not only will they verbalize and express through writing, but also through the medium of art, which transcends conscious thought to the unconscious. In addition to expressing their innermost thoughts, they will learn to appreciate and see the everyday positions of their environment from a different perspective.

The science teachers must be chosen on the basis of their openness to accepting other ways of knowing, a rich science background, and feelings of comfort in working with Native students. The element of presenting two mind sets simultaneously will require patience, especially when paradoxes are being presented, and careful integration of the two is required. This integration will require slow and careful guided reasoning of the more obvious and easily explained aspects of the activity or experience. Planning the learning activities will require questioning by staff, practice with manipulating variables, and testing of possible answers to be learned by the students.

Perhaps the best example to draw on to illustrate how learning will occur is the creation story as told by Joe Friday of Chevak, where a male and a female discover themselves by a riverbank. They find everything they need to make a living arranged along there—clothing, cooking utensils, hunting implements, qayaq, tools, and so forth. They have no notion of what the items are, nor how to use them. They learn what they need to know through a combination of trial and error, imagination, visions, discussion and questioning (i.e., meditation), and spiritual intervention.

The story would be told and the investigative process brought to the fore by student discussion. The ancient story uses discovery and inquiry, espoused by modern educators to be one of the most effective ways of teaching and learning. It enhances immediate learning, later transfer of learning, and improved investigative learning in formal education settings. Science as an investigative process needs to be stressed, more so than the content. Students should recognize that this process is not new but was used by their ancestors. They have to recognize how to question, experiment for possible answers, and if they fail, change the variables and try again. They should learn that failure is a necessary ingredient for success.

Students should know that when people are in touch with nature, they are in touch with Ellam Yua, the Spirit of the Universe. When in touch with It, they are in the realm of science, the world of inquiry and discovery. In order for the Yupiaq to live in harmony with nature, they had to learn the skills to live in and with nature; they had to learn the values of nature for mutual nurturing and sustenance, from which they developed a holistic philosophy of the universe. In light of this, there is no reason for a Yupiaq to have an inadequate self-image and shy away from mathematics and the sciences.

The teacher has to use all the available perceptive and sensory tools of visualization or visual thinking to be applied to the experiences of the students. The environment becomes a laboratory, and thus the teaching is from an ecological perspective. Most students have the ability to see, therefore see images; have a mind, therefore think; and have some degree of ability to draw or doodle. These three faculties are often used by Native adults to arrive at solutions to problems. The empirical data are collected in the mind and serve as the basis for formulating conclusions, which are shaped by the individual's perceptions, values, concepts, philosophy of life, and how he or she relates to the world. Through the millennia, culture has established a way to make the world accessible to reasoned inquiry and discovery, addressing questions of what is real, what is truth, and what is good and beautiful. The resolution to these questions flows and is channeled through science, art, and religion. The natural phenomena in the Yupiaq world are explained in terms of characteristics that are easily observable or experiences involving a high degree of intuitive thought.

This proposal attempts to set the stage, testing out the systematic study of science based on Yupiaq and Western perspectives. My reasoning for this is that it will enhance learning as we are dealing with experiences with which students utilize, consciously or unconsciously, their own culturally derived thinking processes. The mix of the two adds another dimension of comparative analysis and creative thinking. These two are often missing in the modern educational paradigm.

I do not include time schedules or logistical needs, for I feel my effort is to present ideas on how we could carry out a program that encompasses two ways of knowing at the same time. There will be numerous Yupiaq cultural activities interspersed throughout the program, including storytelling, videotapes and films, visiting speakers, Yupiaq dancing, traditional games of skill, men's and women's activities, and arts and crafts to especially express innermost feelings, how they perceive the world to be, what they want it to be, and so forth.

One also needs to develop goals. I propose the following, which will not all be met in a short period of time but should be considered long-range goals:

1. Apply and blend Yupiaq and modern science perspectives
2. Practice effective application of the scientific processes in everyday life
3. Practice flexibility in levels of thinking and foster effective thinking in everyday life
4. Maintain and enhance essential ecological processes and life support systems by using complex scientific technology to

       develop simpler technology in tune with nature

5. Practice Yupiaq conservation for genetic diversity

6. Sustain utilization of species and ecosystems

7. Exercise creative writing and creative applications of the imagination and visualization to improve the natural environment and enhance natural processes of food production

8. Adapt to changing conditions through a blend of Yupiaq (natural) and modern science principles

9. Sustain a network of collaborative thought and effort between disciplines, maintaining a holistic approach at all times

The staff will consist of a "chief," a science teacher, an art teacher, an elderly couple expert in fish camp life, a camp cook, and a maintenance and carver person. The chief will not be the modern corporate-style school administrator, but the servant of the staff and students. She or he will be the person who maintains order by mere presence and age and the person to whom all turn for consultation. The chief will be the one to help maintain individual and collective balance. The camp will be a collaborative effort to attain synergy where the group is greater than its individual members, and the individual within the group is greater than alone. It may sound idealistic; however, I would strive for this, putting our talents together to build esprit de corps and the highest standards of success in self-esteem and achievement. With all these elements in place, we can begin the fish camp science odyssey.

A Fish Camp Science Odyssey Curriculum

Let us begin in the beginning, with the stories of creation as reflected in Yupiaq legend and the Bible, one of many creation myths. The students will be told both creation stories, along with the theory of evolution. The Bible closely parallels our myths, though nothing is written to give either one credence over the other. The other theory, that of evolution, needs to be discussed as a theory of classifying animals and plants based on structural likenesses, but, as with the creation stories, we cannot corroborate the theory through direct observation, but only by conjecture. In the creation stories, man, animals, and things were made by a being and are guided by natural laws to assure survival, thus leading to a holistic view of the world. The theory of evolution is based upon the gift of analytical observation and the resulting perspicacious reasoning ability. Scientists observed, theorized, and checked to see whether experience bore out the theory. These are the two minds of science. The students might be required to write a paper on their understanding of these two systems of thought.

In the Bear-Woman story presented in chapter 2, there are two young people who all of a sudden become conscious of being in a strange environment. Much in the way of food, clothing, cooking utensils, hunting implements, and furs is at their disposal. But what are they? How must they be used? What skills will be needed to replicate items that slowly wear out or are expendable? How might these two young people figure out the purposes of the various items, what they are made of, and how they were made. What is to be their relationship to the world around them? What might have helped them ascertain use? Over a long period of time, what outside help might the two have received? Eventually, how would they determine who they are, their place in the world, and their relationship to everything else? This story provides many topics for discussion and written assignments.

There will need to be much time for introspection. Think about yourself. When do you talk to yourself? What do you call the pictures or images in your mind? Draw a picture of yourself as you see yourself now. Draw another as you would like to be in the future. Draw a picture of your family, including yourself.

After a couple sessions of such activities, begin to consider the scientific method. It is a method for exploring the world around you and where you fit into that world. It is asking questions, finding out what the variables are, manipulating the variables, and testing for possible answers. Go back to the boy and girl in the myth. Was their method for exploring and finding an answer similar to that of a modern-day scientist? What, for instance, do you boys do when your outboard motor or snow machine stops all of a sudden? Or you girls, when you determine to make a clothing item for your six-year-old sister and you have only one square yard of corduroy cloth? Both of you, essentially, use the same inquiry steps to try to resolve your problem. Now make an outline of the steps used by yourself or a member of your family to solve a problem, or by a collective problem-solving task recently in the village. These outlines can then serve as a basis for subsequent discussion.

In the Bear-Woman story, a little robin became the messenger to the despairing woman. Our Yupiaq philosophy presupposes that all plants and animals have spirits. There is nothing wrong with this worldview. No philosophy is solely right! Over a period of several days the students can make forays into the environment to identify as many songbirds as possible and especially to identify and record the call of the robin. With a variable speed player, they can experiment with the songs. Could these songs be a form of communication between like species and to others? Were they disturbed or frightened by a predator such as a hawk? What would make you think so? Is it possible that the robin could have been a messenger? The Yupiaq identify and call the birds, mainly on the basis of their songs. Is this an acceptable way of classifying rather than the criteria from *The Origin of Species*? Who's right? Have the Yupiaq been doing science? Since when?

The songs of the birds, when played back at a slower speed, reveal sounds that we, with our human hearing apparatus, do not discern, but which most likely the birds themselves understand. The students should be asked to find a bird's nest and watch the actions when there is an intruder. When other birds trespass, what are the behavioral changes in the nesting couple? Are you engaged in science? Can slight changes in intonations and sounds in the robin's song convey a message in Yupiaq? Highly probable, though this is conjectural on my part. Animals have helped so many of our people to survive in times of danger through various means that it is hard for me as a Yupiaq to discount the probability.

Ask the elders about the different feathers and what they understand about their functions. Look in the science textbook and see how the modern scientist explains this. What tools does the scientist use to come to a conclusion? How did the Yupiaq come to this conclusion? Were their conclusions similar? How did they know this without modern tools?

In the creation story, what are the intellectual attributes that made the boy and girl successful in solving seemingly insurmountable conundrums about the function of each item? Are these attributes present in our elders? The science teacher? The cook? The president of Chase Manhattan Bank? A Yupiaq hunter? The president of the United States? A Yupiaq housewife? Amazing, to have the same qualifiers for success!

Draw and show how the boy might have felt when he discovered what the "paddle" was to do for him and the kayak. For the girl, draw her expression as she discovered the use of the bone needle and sinew thread. Write an essay on how you feel and how you show it when you are happy or have just completed an assignment successfully.

Take several feet of a brightly colored surveyor's ribbon and tie a weight onto one end. Throw it into the air as high as possible. Wherever it lands, measure and mark an area five feet in radius with the weight as the center. How do you measure this? Within this circle, identify all the plants. Have the elders give the Yupiaq names. Find out what they know about the plants. What do they recognize as being necessary for plant growth? Find some broad-leafed plants and, using black construction paper, cover a whole leaf. Cover half a leaf on another. After three days, test for chemical composition, such as chlorophyll and starch.

This is modern science in action. One can begin to talk about chemical symbols, formulas, and equations. There are 104 elements within our world which make up everything singularly or in various combinations. These are the things that a chemist works with. This is how the chemist determines what a thing is made of, what goes on in the process, and what energy is required for a chemical reaction to happen. They are the ones who have discovered or invented penicillin, nylon, deoxyribonucleic acid (DNA), and so forth. This involves a lot of asking the right questions, researching, communicating, testing theories, manipulating variables, persistence, intuition, and sometimes just plain happy accidents. Many discoveries are of the serendipitous kind—penicillin was one, and the benzene structure derived from a dream was another.

Have the elders demonstrate the traditional means of measurement. Traveling long distances required experience and thought on the part of the traveler, who must think means of travel, currents, load, presence of tides, winds, and means of propulsion. To be properly prepared, it was necessary to estimate distance and how long it would take to get there. The word *cukneq*, or 'measure,' implies visualization and estimation based on comparing something to something else. This includes the available food and how long it will last. It is projecting into the future based on what we are doing and what is available now. Perceptions of space are also shaped by this worldview. The qasegiq becomes the center of a man's space. The house becomes the center for the woman. Material things, spirits, time, people, or plants are all around. The past is important because it shapes identity and provides a lens for viewing space and time.

Since the Yupiaq did not develop research tools as such, the notion *tangruarluki kanginguakluki* (to pretend to see, then to understand) implies much intuition and visualization and thrusts insight into the spiritual realm. Dreams, visions, and spirits working with receptive individuals, especially shamans, help us to understand phenomena that defy rational and analytical explanations. I believe Western science shortchanges itself by disdaining Native American thought. There still remains much that modern science cannot understand or explain in this world. However, it behooves us, the Natives, to work to retain our identity and special lens, while borrowing from the modern scientific technology to enhance our quality of life. As we do this, we must adhere to the natural laws and processes, so that the quality we obtain for ourselves is gained with nature and not at its expense.

Domestication carries with it a notion of ownership, and to this we have subjected only the dog. It is considered to be like people— take care of it and in return it will take care of you. Abuse it, and you cannot expect anything from it. Perhaps our attitude toward domestication will eventually change, especially with respect to agriculture and aquaculture.

The carrying capacity of the land and water is fast approaching maximum utilization because of the increasing population and the ravages of pollution. Since we are studying from an ecological perspective, the students should go to the marshes and bogs to collect vegetation and water samples. This is an important source of nutrients, as well as a repository of pollutants. What do the elders have to say on this? What notions do they have about the food web? How do they know what the various species feed on and who uses them for food? Compare this with Fish and Game teaching materials on food webs.

Of utmost importance to the hunter is the weather. The elders say, "The sun declares what the weather is going to be." "Use your eyes to recognize signs." "Read your environment." For the Yupiaq, the indicators are numerous. Ask the elders to read the weather every day and see how close the predictions are. Then observe the wind direction, the direction of wind changes, cloud formations, the layers of clouds, the wind direction on the surface as compared to the direction of flow of a second layer of clouds, forming clouds over mountains, sunrises and sunsets, sundogs, and the feel of the air. Have the students use modern tools for measurement of wind speed, direction, air pressure, humidity, temperature, and satellite pictures for cloud movement. It is interesting to note when the radio announcer in the morning says that the beautiful weather we are having is contrary to the modern satellite-based weather prediction. Have students observe the weather every day, recording the elders' predictions, as well as recording what actually happens. As elders advise, you get better with experience.

Other signs to ask elders about include trees looking very dark; white or dark clouds forming around mountains; sundogs—red outside, green inside; mittens—red but dark in the inside; northern lights—dark on the underside or red; moon with crescent emptying or upward; stars twinkling; sunrise slow; if the sun slips fast across sky and sets fast, and so forth. The elders say we are making the weather bad and ruining it, because we have lost honor and respect for the Earth. To know our place, our space, is to know it intimately, its weather patterns, its natural features, its plants, its animals, with an openness of mind and sensitivity to subtle changes. This is identity—who you are—the pride of otherness!

These suggestions present many possibilities for writing projects, arts and crafts, social studies, and mapping populations (animal, plant, and man). They lend themselves to ethnoscience projects, such as the qasegiq, with its architecture geared to fit the Yupiaq mind set. The qasegiq is built of all natural materials, it fits into nature, it is nature—heat efficient in winter, cool in the summer. Study the qasegiq architecture, its materials, its place in nature as compared to the schoolhouse. Which would you think would be most cost effective and energy efficient? How would you determine the R-factor of the walls?

In the making of dry fish, study the general purpose uluaq. It is a multiuse tool for everything from delicate to heavy-duty cutting, including cutting through bones. Compute the increase in force (foot-pounds) necessary to cut through bone. In drying fish, follow the energy transformations needed to produce the end product, the dry fish. With the simplest of scientific technology, a delicacy is produced.

Compare the engineering of the traditional dog sled to that of today. Consider the furs used to make parkas, pants, and mukluks. How did the Yupiaq know of the capacity of some furs to absorb radiant energy? How did they learn about the transformation of energy to give warmth? Or that dead air spaces help to retain body heat? Or the reading of weather indicators to predict how cold and long the winter is going to be—a matter of starvation or survival. Or the architecture and engineering used to produce the qayaq, a marvel of a water craft. What gives it structural strength yet flexibility? What is the tensile strength of seal or walrus skin as opposed to aluminum or steel? What about the engineering of the single and double paddles, with the blade being long and slim?

Why? The arrow is aerodynamically superior to many rockets. It served its purpose well for our people. Why was the three-pronged arrow used for birds or fish? For birds on the wing, it was necessary to allow for the speed of the bird and the velocity of the arrow. For shooting fish, how did the Yupiaq allow for refraction and diffraction?

Everything the man and woman had—clothing, hunting equipment, craft tools, and so forth—were custom-made for the individual, personalized for strength, balance, accuracy, and uniqueness of the person. How does this contribute to identity and pride for hunter and provider or food preparer and clothier?

Native people have engaged in highly abstract thinking at the spiritual level, using visualization and blended expression in the art of spiritual and pragmatic forms, for example, masks. The artistic and the practical cannot be readily separated in Yupiaq society.

Western scientific technology has given much to make life easier and longer, but this has not always enhanced the quality of life. The high level of modern living enjoyed by a few is accomplished at the expense of many other people—and of the Earth. We therefore must press for working within the natural laws and processes by which our ultimate relationship with the environment is governed. We can ill afford to continue to do otherwise.

A variation on the Hegelian triad of thesis, antithesis, synthesis is what I propose needs to happen in the teaching of mathematics and the sciences in this fish camp odyssey. The Yupiaq version of knowing can be taught first as the thesis, with the Western version given next as the antithesis. The order of presentation can be modified, depending on the complexity of the subject being studied, the comprehension of the material, the readiness of the students, and whether the students have a good understanding of the basic principles involved. It is up to the teacher to gauge readiness. Once both approaches have been presented and considered, then the students may begin to search for a synthesis. To actualize the thought process, the students may have to be walked through by the teachers and elders with closely guided reasoning to incorporate the two mind sets on the basis of discovery and inquiry.

It is imperative that the students learn basic scientific principles and technologies, so they can use this understanding to develop simpler, more nature-sensitive technologies than the Western ones. For example, the housing in our region is a scourge to our people. Have the students review the technology of existing materials and structures, examining the advantages and disadvantages of each. Have them think about the natural materials and structures, with their advantages and disadvantages. Have them think about the natural materials available from their environment. Using the scientific method, they might then consider the following problem:

Problem: Our original houses were derived from and a part of nature. What materials and designs can we use to develop a structure using natural materials and incorporating modern technology?

Materials available: sand, peat, thirteen varieties of bushes, sod, water, sunlight, iron rods, cement, resins, studs, plywood, lumber, glass, etc.

Known: Elders remember how the qasegiqs were constructed.

Experiment: Construct a traditional house using only natural material.

1. Selection of site
2. Dig into the ground three to four feet deep
3. Construct a framework out of driftwood, using no nails, only notches
4. Cut blocks of sod for insulation. Place on wood or planks. Blocks are placed with the vegetation on the inside. Plants grow naturally on the outside.
5. Make a skylight with removable seal or walrus intestine cover

Review and analyze the modern architect-designed house. Look at materials, site, elevation, insulation, heat sources, etc.

Alternative designs to investigate: design a container and compress peat for forming into bricks. Sun dry some, dry others in an oven. When dried and ready, arrange several bricks approximately 4' x 4' upright. Arrange one with no adhesive between bricks, one with a resin adhesive between each. The bricks now need something to give structural strength and protection from the elements. Try covering one with a layer of cement on all sides, another with tar, one with tar on the outside and with cement on the inside, one with cement on outside and resin on the inside. After several days, test for strength using those guidelines deemed important by the villagers.

Findings by category: What is the next step? How? Water seepage control? Test conditions for strength, durability, R-factor, etc.?

Challenge: Can you develop a cheaper, more heat efficient, and structurally strong house suited for the cold climates?

The above lesson, which has been successfully implemented in a coastal village, provides an idea of the possibilities for synthesizing a variety of approaches to come up with better solutions to everyday problems, including the problem of making science education relevant to village students. Begin to think of other ways the students can use their Native and modern intricate knowledge to devise simpler technologies. The possibilities are vast and varied.

Another teaching approach might be to teach the concepts of elasticity, thrust, force, speed, velocity, aerodynamics, inertia, momentum, foot-pounds, trajectory, resistance, buoyancy, pressure, stabilizers, center of gravity, payload, acceleration, deceleration, drag, and so on, by using the bow and arrow and qayaq. Begin the class studies with the bow. How does it provide thrust for the arrow? Here you can discuss potential and kinesthetic power. What determines the power of the bow? What might the Native hunter do to increase this? The hunter strung the bow only when he was ready to use it. Why? The hunter would look for driftwood that was straight. He would then cut off a piece whose length was determined by his height and reach. He would then split it, carefully following the wood grain. Why do you suppose he did this? Using his *mell'gag*, or curved knife, he would fashion and smooth its surface. He would then add a stone or flint point and feathers on the other end. What are some scientific principles he has to be aware of to do this? The technology is simple, to be sure; but he does it with care and uses all naturally available products. He may even place on it the family crest, the signature of his family, which clearly identifies the owner.

The students could research several different arrow point designs used for different purposes. Other things they might ask the elders include how they knew and allowed for refraction. Ask them how the warriors were trained to use the bow and arrow and how they were to defend against incoming arrows. To do this, estimation of distance, speed, and time have to be calculated in the mind in fractions of a second.

Next, take a look at the architecture and engineering of the qayaq. It is streamlined, built for strength, uses natural products, is light for transportability, and it has a high capacity for payload and stability. Again, the size is determined by the owner-to-be: it is custom-made. The covering is made of sealskin or walrus skin. The skins are sewn onto the framework. When it is finished, the seams and skins are coated with a mixture of seal oil and peat. The mixture is first allowed to age. Why do you suppose this is or was done? Several years ago, a group of Danish scientists tested out how seaworthy and strong a craft made in this way was. Their findings were that it was most seaworthy. The skin, in its moist condition, becomes resilient and flexible and has better tensile strength than aluminum or steel of equal thickness. The framework adds to the strength, as each piece is tied to the ribbing with skin thongs that get elastic when moist. It is highly resilient yet has great strength.

Now you can contrast the bow and arrow and qayaq with the modern ballistic missile and rocket power for controlled flight. The power source is different, with man-made, highly combustible fuel. Its architecture and engineering employs the principles applied to the bow and arrow and the qayaq. However, the materials and power sources differ a great deal. The former use natural materials and are constructed mindful of spirits and natural processes. The latter have taken a different path. Analytical thinking has been applied through the scientific method to derive a highly complex machine of great power that can travel long distances. The scientific principles and applications are the same. The former has chosen a very simple survival technology to assure life for oneself and the Earth. It appears very simple from the modern point of view but is very complex if considered from the panoramic viewpoint of maintaining an equilibrium for all life. We must train young minds into mathematics and the sciences, so that they can use a blend of these very intricate scientific technologies to develop more appropriate technologies for survival and to begin to undo the damage that has been wrought upon our planet Earth.

The first two people in our origin story used the scientific method too, so it is not new to our Native people. Men use it every time they plan a hunting trip. Women use it every time they go out berry picking to provide for the winter months.

Whether derived from experiences in the fish camp setting described above or from textbooks in a school classroom, mathematics and science curricula can be approached in a way that integrates Yupiaq and Western knowledge systems and the methods by which they are derived. A teacher, whether Native or not, can develop explanations and experimentations by asking elders, young educated people, and the students themselves how something studied was or can be applied in village life. I believe this process, if used honestly and creatively, can enhance the self-image of the young person, first as a human being of worth, and secondly as a Native person. The student can then strengthen this Nativeness with a valid need for otherness but with a natural respect for others.

The mystery of mathematics and science should begin to dissolve when students understand that their ancestors have been applying scientific principles for millennia and that these are very much a part of their everyday life. Both Yupiaq and Western scientific knowledge and principles are a part of the whole body of human knowledge and skills and must be approached from that perspective.

From the Yupiaq Fish Camp to Gaia

In teaching students to become ecologically aware and to live with nature, we have to go back to the "time-honored pattern of the elements of life: earth, air, fire, water and spirit" (Mills 1990:xii). The students must come to understand each element that contributes to life, how our modern life is endangering its life-giving processes, and what we might do to prevent or at least stem the destructive aspects of human enterprises. The Yupiaq creation legends, stories, rituals, and ceremonies attest to the interconnectedness of the human to all things of the earth. Whatever the human being does to change the environment has an effect in the future. The ecological system is very delicate and interdependent. James Lovelock's "Gaia hypothesis is that together the planet, its life-forms, and its atmosphere are interacting and mutually creating, and have some of the properties of living tissue; that the earth is like an organism" (Mills 1990:5).

The Yupiaq desire would be to have this ecological knowledge clearly presented and demonstrated by teachers, students, elders, and other community members. As Stephanie Mills points out (1990), the Yupiaq knowledge can be broadened, strengthened, and given more detail by incorporating modern scientific knowledge without changing the original Yupiaq understanding. The Yupiaq people have been aware for a long time of the destructiveness of the modern world with its emphasis on controlling and making money from the world's natural resources. The modern world's bifurcation of the earth's natural resources into renewable and nonrenewable has contributed to a mentality oriented toward refining resources into manufactured items with built-in obsolescence. This includes new-model automobiles, clothes with changing styles and fads, and throwaway packaging. To support this lifestyle, we engage in over-fishing, decimating buffalo, clear-cutting forests, and draining aquifers. The modern world is becoming aware of these excesses and demanding more information on negative changes on earth and ultimately will have to recognize that ecology is a major force in the economy as well as our future on this planet.

Air, as Mills indicates, is the "Earth's enveloping atmosphere[,] is the cauldron of planet-girdling currents of wind, humidity, and temperature, the arena of tornadoes, blizzards, and drought. The weather is a mix of water and air driven by fire (in the form of solar radiation). Impeded and rerouted by Earth's land forms, given its dynamic by temperature differentials and the Earth's rotation, weather governs our lives. Over evolutionary time each living thing has developed a specific relationship to the weather and climate" (1990:62–63). The Yupiaq people in distant time knew much about weather and the permutations that controlled their activities. Now there is occurring an atmospheric decomposition from industrialization and the teeming world population. Yupiaq people say that the weather conditions have changed. What are the chemical agents for these changes? What can you as teacher, student, elder, or community member do to ameliorate the situation?

Mills further puts fire "at the heart of the Earth, just as fire is the heart of our solar system, and the heart and hearth of human culture" (1990:91). Fire is necessary to cleanse the body, heart, and soul. Fire is used to give heat and light for the home, for giving light for performing ceremonies, for burning old growth to make room for new growth, providing new homes and reinvigorating plants and animals, for giving smoke to preserve meat, and many other uses. Fire today is used to create energy for homes and industry using wood, coal, oil, or nuclear fuels. Fire is used to refine metals to make various tools and machines. Fire is used to propel our automobile, snow machine, outboard motor, airplane, and so on. Besides fuel, what is required to make fire? How is fire contributing to decomposition of the air and pollution of the earth? What are alternative energy sources?

According to Mills, "Water is so everywhere-present, and such a commonplace, that its gifts seem almost limitless. Water is the only substance on Earth that exists in all three physical states—solid, liquid, and gaseous. . . . Earth is integral—the biosphere runs on water, sunlight, and minerals" (1990:123). Water is absolutely necessary for life. What has the modern human being done that is destroying water? Is this a renewable resource in modern eyes? In some instances, especially underground, water is fast becoming a nonrenewable resource. How is this coming about? Our continents are usually divided into countries, and the countries are divided into states, provinces, districts, or in some other fashion. This may be advantageous for governance, but does it create problems of inappropriate resource utilization? Why?

Spirit, Mills says, is "something larger and more mysterious than the individual self. As humans, our conception of soul and psyche is largely shaped by the human mind. However, with the image of Gaia, and our deepening understanding of ecology, it seems the life force itself shows intelligence—mind in nature" (1990:157). The Yupiaq people have always had this in their consciousness as a way of life. They have held and acknowledge a force greater than the human being which flows through each being as a soul of its own. Rituals and ceremonies were created to show honor and reverence for the Ellam Yua, and to center oneself to maintain or regain balance, ordering one's life. The tetrahedral model of the Yupiaq worldview tries to show this.

How can we use these five elements to teach science? And beyond, for it must not stop there. The teachers must coordinate their activities so that language arts, social studies, arts and crafts, Yupiaq language, mathematics, and the sciences are all connected. We must use the environment, elders, legends and stories, rituals and ceremonies, and Yupiaq artifacts to teach. Mills teaches that "Learning is a function of a nurturant relationship, and the living world is the greatest teacher. The genius of traditional peoples is that they teach their lifeways continually, and by a variety of means, from cradle songs to pervasive symbolic connotation attached to seemingly commonplace objects, to epic creation tales, to ritual offerings in specific places, to legitimating the authority of all elders in the tribe to teach the correct lifeway, the lifeway appropriate to place" (1990:159). This is valuable wisdom for people to reconnect with the earth. The Yupiaq students will become motivated to learn from their distant ancestors and the elders of today.

Summary

Yupiaq science education should attempt to take the Native student as far intellectually as possible. This means that the student understands how her or his own people make sense of the world and how they have developed their technology. The Yupiaq people are doing science when involved in subsistence activities. They know about flora and fauna; they have their own way of meteorology, knowledge of physics, chemistry, earth science, astronomy, the sacred, and the individual's inner world. The Yupiaq explanations of natural phenomena must be explained in Yupiaq terms, and not just in Western terms. I say this because when I have tried to get elders to present their knowledge in Western terms and ideas, confusion seems to result. Explaining an eddy along the river for placing a setnet must be handled in the Yupiaq way of understanding, at least initially. This can then be explained in modern terms, such as speed of flow, resistance, turgidity, and tide tables. Let the teacher, students, elders, parents, and bilingual and teacher aides determine in what ways the modern explanation adds to the Yupiaq explanation and understanding. All learning should start with what the student and community know and are using in everyday life. The Native student will become more motivated to learn science when it is based on something useful and suitable to the livelihood of the Yupiaq people.

The student should become scientifically literate—that is, know what scientists do, know something about the impact of science on society, or know what some basic terms and concepts mean. The science teacher need not try to prepare students only for advanced work at the university. Picking up on science and doing well at the university level seems to be based more on the intelligence or ability and motivation of the student than on prior knowledge. The students must be shown first how mathematics, science, and technology are dependent on each other and bear on their everyday lives.

Mathematics, science, and technology are human concerns and thus are subject to advantages, limitations, use, misuse, and abuse. Together, they have enabled new surgical methods, medicines, engineering designs for automobiles and planes, vast storage of information, rapid transfer of money and material, nanotechnology, trajectory to the moon, nuclear energy, and new weapons of war. Yupiaq numbering and sciencing are nature mediated and thus are not abstractions of the human mind, as are modern math, science, and technology.

In the Yupiaq sense of the sacred there exists a nucleus of spirituality and beauty graphically depicted by myths, legends, songs and dances, and masks and other artifacts in which respect and beauty are inscribed into words and wood adorned with natural ornaments and paints. Yupiaq science contributed to thinking, problem solving, and preparing for the tasks of life and gave to the practitioner personal empiricism and thus a sense of self-reliance and self-determination.

The old manuals and laboratory experiments as we know them are no longer adequate for the study of science. One cannot effectively study the ecological systems in the laboratory or grow a balanced aquarium or terrarium in the classroom or study the effects of sewage and garbage. Holistic science lacks the adaptability to the standard laboratory format that the old science topics fit.

So it behooves science teachers to take a look at Native ways of science—patient long-term observation in natural settings, reflection individually and in groups, testing of theories, and attention to intuitive thought from the natural and the spiritual worlds. The latter give a moral basis to Yupiaq science. The old adage that nothing in the world is constant except the process of constant change has always been foremost in the Yupiaq mind and should continue. We need to recognize that the Western techno-mechanistic worldview is no longer adequate or appropriate and that a paradigmatic shift toward a holistic worldview is necessitated by a deteriorating global situation.

Using the five elements of earth, air, fire, water, and spirit as teaching tools will allow elders to contribute to the renewal of knowledge. Teachers, students, and community members will come to know and understand the Yupiaq philosophy of life and worldview, with its language, values, and methodologies for teaching. They will begin to know their place in space and time intimately. They will begin to know themselves both inwardly and outwardly. In using math, science, and technology, Yupiaq people would learn what science is all about, the impact that science and technology have had on their lives, what a scientist does, and scientific terms and concepts peculiar to their world. From such an undertaking, all humankind would benefit.

Conclusion

Using a Yupiaq worldview as a base, this study has attempted to provide a conceptual framework for rethinking what we teach in schools and how we teach it, particularly as it pertains to science. Central to this Yupiaq-based framework is the need to understand the interrelatedness of all things in the universe, including the natural, human, and spiritual realms. In teaching students about the five elements of life—earth, air, fire, water and spirit—it is important that they understand that each is a sacred gift to the life-giving forces of Mother Earth, and that all are necessary for life on earth to survive. Together, they make it possible for creation on earth to continue. The Yupiaq people have honored and respected these gifts in their rituals and ceremonies. In return, the earth has provided homes for people, animals, and plants. We can all expand our knowledge and enrich our lives by seeking to better understand the Yupiaq people's perceptions and behaviors in relation to the natural and spiritual worlds, which have served for millennia to sustain their lives.

The modern schools are not teaching students how to live a sustainable life. Rather, they transmit a lot of information to the students, but without also showing them how to convert that information into useful knowledge for making a living. Another step is required for people, individually and collectively, to sort out what is usable knowledge that can be transformed into the wisdom necessary to not only make a living, but to make a life. The many machines, modern tools, and vaunted computers are not enough to teach us a lifeway that nurtures the soul. It is important, therefore, that we find ways to use the elemental spirit, values, and cultures of indigenous peoples, such as the Yupiaq, to create a new lifeway that achieves the harmony and balance necessary for a quality of life that is sustainable.

To achieve this, we must come to recognize that the make-up of the world is nonlinear, and that as a result we will never fully understand and exercise control over everything in the universe. We must also realize and appreciate that in modern scientific and technological endeavors, mathematics, science, and technology are interrelated, as are all other disciplines. Science education must, therefore, become aligned with the common philosophical thread, or the "distant memory," as it is called by N. Scott Momaday in one of his pioneering autobiographical novels, *The Way to Rainy Mountain* (1969). All peoples of the earth began from this vista, and we must return to it for attaining a new consciousness and a sustainable life.

To begin to understand these phenomena, the sacred gifts of each of the five elements must be understood, along with the exploitative human activities that contribute to our despiritualization through the reduction of the earth's life-giving qualities. In order to be holistic, the educational activities associated with each element must include Yupiaq language and culture, language arts, mathematics, social studies, arts and crafts, and the sciences. All must be interrelated, just as all is interrelated at the fish camp, and as all of earth is interrelated. Like the lessons from the many myths, such as the Bear-Woman story, all phenomena are dynamic, ever changing, and, like the myth, mystical.

Continued assault on our planet Earth is an assault on our personal and collective freedom. As the people and product pollution continue to encroach upon our lands, more laws, rules, and regulations are enacted to try to mitigate their adverse effects, which cause physical, emotional, psychological, and earthly pains. These very laws, enacted to help make the situation tolerable, also serve to isolate people from nature. As a result, a lonely cry ensues, heard not only from indigenous peoples, but from many people globally. Among the Yupiaq people there is an attempt at reviving a sense of sacredness in being, thinking, acting and doing, and restoring a sense of place, where a lifeway that goes beyond making a living can be restored. This can be a gift of life from the Yupiaq people. The ultimate gift is that of the spirit. This gift is embodied in the Yupiaq language, mythology, rituals, and ceremonies. Through it is taught the "correct lifeway, a lifeway appropriate to place" (Mills 1990:159). It is to that end, and beginning, that this work has been dedicated.

Tuaii, am'llegiuk. Quyana!

Appendix
Research Considerations

Research can be broadly defined as "an attempt to find out about something or find a solution to a problem" (Eisner 1991:66). Science is a way of knowing and doing things. New ways of knowing and doing have been brought into the lives of the Yupiaq people through contact with Western society. Confusion is everywhere. The Yupiaq have had very little input into the construction of their new world, so the methods for this type of study have to be carefully planned and executed, always open to possible modification to fit the village situations and local perceptions (Chrisjohn, Towson, & Peters 1988). What follows is an account of the considerations that went into my preparation for fieldwork and some retrospective reflections on the fieldwork experience. The actual results are reflected in the presentation of data in subsequent chapters.

Max van Manen (1990:35) points out that much modern educational research suffers from

1. Confusing pedagogical theorizing with other discipline-based forms of discourse
2. Tending to abstraction and thus losing touch with the lifeworld of the living child
3. Failing to see the general erosion of pedagogic meaning from the lifeworld

As I prepared for my research, I posed the following as some of the salient questions that had to be kept in mind to try to minimize the above limitations:

1. Is the research problem observable and operational in the Yupiaq world?
2. Is the research problem appropriate in the mind of the villagers?
3. Can the research problem be approachable, touchable, or addressable with the proposed methodology?
4. Do the villagers consider the methodology appropriate?
5. Will documentary and village input be readily available during my visits?
6. How will I know that my perceptions and interpretations are accurate?
7. How do I alleviate cultural and scientific biases?

The research design that follows addresses these questions, in some cases explicitly and others implicitly.

It is toward the (re)integration of the human, spiritual, and natural, the Native and the Western worlds, in the lives and education of Native people that this study is directed. What is needed as a first step in this process is a study of and by Native people, examining their values, practices, attitudes, and views in relation to their traditional and contemporary ecological perspective. It has been my intent to participate in and observe life in a Yupiaq Eskimo community and fish camp to identify the varied ways in which people incorporate traditional and Western knowledge in their daily lives and determine how they have been able to reconcile the seemingly antithetical values reflected in each. Can Western teachings and Yupiaq practices be understood and taught through a common epistemological framework? Of particular concern is the application and acquisition of traditional and Western scientific knowledge in the school and in the everyday life of the community, because such practices are most readily observable and embody many of the elements that make up the Yupiaq worldview.

Research Setting

I have chosen the Yupiaq Eskimo fish camp, community, and school setting to examine the ways in which Yupiaq people make sense of the world in which they live. The summer fish camp season is a time of happiness, warm weather, and orderly Yupiaq industry. It also presents a cornucopia of traditional and modern technologies. Although the Yupiaq people do not always have technical names for the natural processes involved, the annual fish camp routines reflect the most concentrated situation in which they use many sophisticated scientific principles in activities such as preparing food, catching and preserving fish, reading river currents and tides, assessing weather and wind conditions, utilizing solar energy, adapting to seasonal transformations, and classifying plants, fishes, and animals.

These principles are an inherent part of daily life in the fish camp. In the natural context of the camp environment, Yupiaq people feel they are in the realm of science, the world of inquiry, and the process of discovery. People need to learn how to live in harmony with nature. The secrets of nature have to be learned for mutual nurturing and sustenance and to develop a holistic view of the universe (Murchie 1981).

In the fish camp, the whole environment becomes the laboratory, and thus all teaching and learning is drawn from an ecological perspective. The sensory data that are collected in the mind are used to formulate conclusions based on values, perspectives, philosophy of life, and relations to the world. Over thousands of years, the Yupiaq culture has established a way to make the world accessible to reasoned inquiry and discovery, including ponderous questions about what is real, what is truth, and what is good and beautiful. This knowledge flows and is channeled through Native science, art, and practice of the sacred. Natural phenomena in the Native world are explained in terms of characteristics that are easily observable or in terms of experiences involving a high degree of intuitive thought (Cornell 1986).

In an effort to gain sufficient insight into the Yupiaq understanding and practice of "science" to be able to formulate an approach to science education that incorporates the kinds of principles outlined above, I observed and documented the behaviors and related thinking that are reflected in the day-to-day affairs of the community and the subsistence activities of the summer fish camp. These observations were then juxtaposed against the ways in which science is taught to Yupiaq children in the local school, in an effort to identify points of similarity and difference that can serve as the basis for an integrative approach to the teaching of science for Native people.

Methodology

As a member of the Yupiaq society, I worked from the inside as a participant-observer. I became an active participant with the people at the fish camp, but with constant attention to overt as well as subtle uses of, and comments about, traditional and modern tools and practices. I was raised by a Yupiaq grandmother and experienced seasonal trips for various hunting and trapping activities at an early age. I was taught many of the Yupiaq values of respect for others and nature. I also have an undergraduate major and have taught in the biological sciences, so I have an academic understanding of Western science and the scientific method, with its emphasis on objectivity. However, my elementary, high school, and college education convinced me for many years that modernity was the only way to go. It was only in the last two decades that I began to realize that I was living contrary to my upbringing as a Yupiaq. I have since been searching for a synthesis between the two ways of understanding the world.

I grew up in a traditional village but have also worked in the management of nonprofit and profit corporations on behalf of the Yupiaq people. I worked for two and a half years with the Lower Kuskokwim School District as director of the Native Education Department; my position required that I work with a twenty-seven-member parent committee. It further required that I travel to each of the twenty-six villages at least once a year and at any other time on request. I felt I had excellent rapport with most villagers. I believe I understand how the Yupiaq think and perceive the world, and I speak the language; so I can understand Yupiaq people on their own terms. It is these skills that have allowed me to penetrate beyond the external veneer of the Yupiaq worldview and gain some of the deeper understandings that are often hidden to persons outside a culture.

The research process needs to go beyond the limits of sciences, which are built around bodies of knowledge that are restricted to observable objects of the earth. This so-called objective knowledge, which is based on factual observation of phenomena, constricts original thought. In Yupiaq thought there is a similar idea, translated as seeing without feeling. In Western thought, the objective way of knowing has the greatest value. Subjective knowledge is considered less reliable because it is not verifiable through the senses. The Yupiaq word *tangruarluku*, which means 'to see with the mind's eye,' transcends that which we can perceive with our endosomatic sense makers and illustrates how a Native perspective may provide a way of bridging the so-called mythical subjective world and the objective scientific world. To give credence to the range of phenomena that will need to be addressed from both the Yupiaq and Western perspectives, it is necessary, therefore, that both modes of inquiry and sense making be incorporated.

Interaction, observations, and informal interviews with villagers revealed the cultural beliefs, artifacts, and inherent knowledge used in the fish camp. The process included probing in appropriate cultural domains to try to tease out the subtle patterns and meanings of verbal and physical activities. How do the villagers understand scientific principles? Why do they carry out certain activities the way they do? Has past science education in school contributed to their knowing what to do and the skills needed to succeed in certain instances? How do the villagers pass on their knowledge and skills? How has their relationship to the life-giving ecological system changed? Are there any differences between the beliefs and practices of the older and the younger generations? Through the pursuit of information that addresses these kinds of questions in a fish camp setting, I obtained an insight into the Yupiaq scientific view of the world.

On the other hand, to get an idea of what and how the school attempts to teach students in the sciences required the close examination and content analysis of curricular materials, textbooks, and science manuals, as well as observation of and interviews with teachers. Having taught science for many years, I had a preconceived notion of what to expect. However, science curricula have changed during the years I have been in the classroom, and circumstances can vary from one school to the next. So I had to find out what kinds of scientific knowledge are being taught, how each succeeding grade is introduced to new scientific principles, what kinds of experiments and equipment are being utilized, and most importantly, how the teachers and students view the relationship between school-taught and Yupiaq science.

I conducted formal interviews with teachers to find out how they use the textbooks and manuals, whether they have students relate science to their own environment, whether they make use of science projects and science fairs, and to what extent local knowledgeable people are incorporated in the lessons. All these questions and others that teachers, local people, and students bring up give valuable information as to what goes on during the teaching of science in school. I also conducted open-ended, informal discussions to identify areas not anticipated in the formal interviews. I maintained a daily journal at all times and used audiotapes when permitted. Through these data-gathering processes, I assembled appropriate information to gain insight into the domains of science teaching, learning, and practice in the school and community.

I obtained the consent and cooperation of the Yupiit Nation Tribal Council and Board of Education to carry out the study. The results have been made available to all council and board members. Prior consent and support from the community opened the doors of the village and school to aid the research (Cohen 1982).

Background and Biases of the Researcher

I am Yupiaq, born and raised in the village of Bethel, Alaska. The village's Yupiaq name is *Mamterilleq*, 'a place of many smoke houses.' Having been raised by a Yupiaq-speaking grandmother, I am familiar with the values, customs, and ways of the Yupiaq. I speak the Yupiaq language. During the years since leaving high school, I have lived intermittently in both the Yupiaq and modern worlds. My postsecondary education has been mainly from the University of Alaska-Fairbanks, with the last three years at the University of British Columbia, so the university schooling has been a part of my education, as well as "schooling for qualification" (Kashoki 1982:32). The majority of my graduate education has been from the perspective of the Western middle-class intellectuals' world, which differs markedly from the Yupiaq's perspective and consciousness (Berger 1976).

By influencing the avenues of new thought and direction, especially in situations where the instructors and classes have espoused that there is only one way of doing things, my academic background may have been an impediment to my proposed research (Fahim 1982; Guyette 1983; Kashoki 1982; Lindblom & Cohen 1979; Nakane 1982). However, it was imperative that I try to use all to my advantage. By careful thinking and consulting with the villagers, I attempted to see which methods worked, which needed modification, and which were inappropriate (Petersen 1982). Netting states that "anthropologists must learn some new skills and call on other sciences for expert help" (1986:103), and I would add that they need to learn new skills from sciences of indigenous peoples. This says to me that I must always question my training and be mindful that I may be inadvertently exporting cognitive content and methods from my adopted culture in my efforts to reinterpret and understand my original culture (Berger 1976). It has been argued that many Western research methods and theories are flawed or incomplete when applied to other cultures (Madan 1982). Being mindful of this means that as I assumed the responsibility of researcher, I did not leave my Yupiaq heritage behind and adopt only the vocabulary and concepts of the modern world as my own (Deloria 1991a). If Spradley is correct in stating that "culture is a tool for solving problems" (1979:201), then I am hopeful that I too shall overcome these impediments.

I gathered data on things that I saw, heard, or had pointed out to me by villagers. Especially, I sought to identify ways in which two different worldviews are made to articulate. A worldview is a composite of ideas that give people a way of picturing "sheer reality, their concept of nature, of self, of society. It is the underlying attitude toward themselves and their world" (Geertz 1973:127). This case study was difficult for various reasons. I was dealing with the Yupiaq, human beings who hold thoughts, attitudes, and emotions as cultural artifacts (Geertz 1973). Just how does one go about selecting methods of observing, listening, and interpreting the Yupiaq thoughts, actions, and words? The Yupiaq people have established an innovative self-determining Yupiit Nation, which is asserting their claim of having a fundamental right to alternatives to the state-mandated municipal village government (Kashoki 1982). This knowledge alone should be an advantage for me because I am trying to use that same right for asserting the presence and assessing the effects of multiple forms of consciousness.

School classrooms have been referred to as "hostile environments" (Chrisjohn, Towson, & Peters 1988:257). Native students have used several ways of adapting to this situation. The individual student can adapt by passive resistance, can unconditionally surrender to modern schooling, can surrender on his own terms, or, after having left school, can go back with the intent of legitimizing informal knowledge. The latter is referred to as "creative adaptation" (Chrisjohn, Towson, & Peters 1988:262). Native students' perceptions of schooling may be affected by the opinions held by their parents. Some parents may feel that their school experience was absolutely awful or have the belief that academic success has no bearing on real life or believe education makes Native people less Native (Chrisjohn, Towson, & Peters 1988). These are what I experienced as the weighty reasons for my choice of participant-observation, so that I could listen, talk, and visually evaluate what goes on in the village. This is an important concept if I am to understand the situation described by the above authors. By attempting to visually discover meaning in the Yupiaq world, I am avoiding the use of conventional written reports whose results do not always match reality. Among the Native students, the use of various tests often take on a different function from what they are purportedly measuring (Chrisjohn, Towson, & Peters 1988). The tests can become a barrier. Just introducing them can have a negative affect on how the Native student performs, adapts, or maladapts to the testing situation. This is my reason for shying away from the use of official reports as a primary source of data.

I will use three sources of information. The first is through observing Yupiaq behaviors in their daily lives. The second is listening to and paying particular attention to the content of their conversation. The third is looking at the use of "modern artifacts" in the form of housing, tools, museum archives, written tribal government, and school board reports and minutes, curricula, textbooks, and so forth.

In this case study, I comprehensively studied a small Yupiaq community of 385. The study took place in the village and at the fish camps, where I was an insider while also being a participant-observer (Spradley 1980). Participant observation allowed me to experience the activities directly, to get a feel for them, and to record my own perceptions (Eisner 1991; Freilich 1970; Guyette 1983; Hall 1988; Pelto & Pelto 1978; Shug & Beery 1984; Spradley 1979; Spradley 1980). Depending on the need of the moment, I varied the method of observation. For instance, I made broadly descriptive observations from the time the Yupiaq fisherman landed on the beach of the fish camp to the care and handling of fish by all family members and through to the completion of the activity. At times, I looked at the activities of the women only; therefore my observation became focused, or I watched how each species of fish was split and noted the differences, thus utilizing selective observation (Spradley 1980).

The description of an activity should be an attempt to clarify the reasons that the action is done the way it is. In my case, I tried to gain a better understanding of how the Yupiaq and modern ways of knowing and doing are made to work together in everyday life and whether compromises are made between them or if one is favored over the other. This requires rigorous recording of things seen and heard for later interpretation (Geertz 1973; Pelto & Pelto 1978). The important thing in the description is not the characteristics or traits of the culture bearers (Yupiaq), but the systematic search for relationships in the cognitive maps of the observed (Netting 1986; Pelto & Pelto 1978). Yupiaq people are not only map readers, but also map makers. Their cognitive maps are coding devices built from and adapted to the values, customs, and traditions of their own Yupiaq culture (Netting 1986; Spradley 1980). It is for me to figure out the relationships between behaviors and why these are generated.

Cultural information was gleaned from the words and actions of the Yupiaq in the fish camp. By writing it down, I am preserving what otherwise might have passed away into history. I am trying to capture both the word and the act and fix it into written form so that it can be preserved for future generations (Geertz 1973; Van Maanen 1988). This means that I decoded the words or actions of the Yupiaq and recoded them into English, which then becomes a microscopic representation of Yupiaq behavior (Geertz 1973; Van Maanen 1988). This process becomes problematic, however, because I cannot represent the Yupiaq except on my own terms (Van Maanen 1988). I have three roles when entering the village. I have a professional role, which requires that I uphold the values and standards required of the profession. I have a bureaucratic role as an assistant professor of the University of Alaska. This means that I operate being mindful of the policies and norms of the institution. And last, I have a client orientation, which requires that I must always be very much aware of the Yupiaq needs (Guyette 1983; Hau'ofa 1982). Jack Rothman advises a mixed orientation as most conducive to practical effectiveness (1974). I determined the degrees of mix myself to fit the situation.

By the end of the fieldwork, I had many microscopic Yupiaq representations that were contextualized for analysis. Clifford Geertz puts it succinctly: "Cultural analysis is guessing at meanings, assessing the guesses, and drawing explanatory conclusions from the better guesses, not discovering the Continent of Meaning and mapping out its bodiless landscape" (1973:20). I, as an insider, should have a better chance than most to come upon a closer or more accurate interpretation.

Why a better chance? I already have more in-depth understanding of the particular research problem because I am Yupiaq; therefore, I have much in common with the people I am studying. This is a research problem that comes from familiarity with living the conditions and the problems experienced by Yupiaq people (Barnes 1982; Guyette 1983; Petersen 1982).

As a researcher and as a Yupiaq, I had to be involved with the community to gain the respect and trust of the villagers (Pelto 1965). I had to be honest—direct, clear, and straightforward. I tried to accomplish these directions by continually being aware of what I was doing and, especially, what I was saying. I had to think things through before uttering words, because my words, as well as the things I did, had to match the feelings or intentions I wanted to convey to people (Wilson 1969).

Words have power to change, transform, heal, and to harm; they must be used very carefully. Words are so much a part of human beings and the product of the human being's conceptual world that one must pay close attention (Wilson 1969:129). One should keep in mind that words have subjective and intuitive power as well as objective meanings. It was necessary to establish rapport so that I could be looked on as an honorable person with whom people can share things publicly, confidentially among a group of insiders such as a Native Youth Club, secretly within a closed group, or between two people sharing intimate thoughts and feelings (Freilich 1970). This rapport allowed me to become my own research tool (Eisener 1991; Spradley 1980). It helped me to become more sensitive to the interests and sensibilities of the Yupiaq (Hau'ofa 1982; Spradley 1979).

In the case of those Yupiaq who did not know me very well, we had to go through the rapport stages as depicted by Spradley (1979). They experienced some apprehension or uncertainty about why this Yupiaq person had showed up in their village. After this phase came exploration, a time when they listened to what I said, observed what I did, and began to ask to find out what I was all about, what I knew, and what I wanted from their village. A mutual trust was established. People who trusted me are willing to be associated with me and consent to my questions when they conclude that I mean well. They allowed me to be around them, listening and observing. This led to all villagers participating as informants, a reciprocal relationship between them and myself. The informant is the villager who will be my guide to sense-making markers for meanings of words or actions according to the world they have constructed.

Rapport made it easier for this research project to become "ours," because the approval and changes to the research question and methodology came from within the community (Guyette 1983). We gained constructive motivation with the knowledge the villagers are a necessary element of the research. Constructive motivation is an attitude of wanting to do the very best we can, so that the desired end result will be brought to fruition (Hardwick 1991). We learned from each other during the process of investigation. I insisted on and enlisted villager participation by appealing to the people's sense of community responsibility and by using their collective creativity for problem solving. The more villagers I involved in information gathering, analysis, and understanding in order to arrive at a solution or recommendation, the broader and more in-depth knowledge I could accumulate (Hardwick 1991). I let them know early in the project that I did not have a single methodology that would work in the village, and therefore, I had no easy solutions or answers. I may be a professional, but knowledge production is not delegated only to professionals. Knowledge production is being done daily by the villagers. In fact, it is a mistake for professionals to exclude the ordinary knowledge of ordinary people derived by common sense, casual empiricism, or thoughtful speculation (Lindblom & Cohen 1979). The more people involved in knowledge production and in the process of analysis leading to problem solving, the more likely we will generate the most accurate interpretation (Guyette 1983; Hall 1988).

Many sources of tension can cause one to become ineffective. Most often these tensions are caused by cultural differences (Guyette 1983; Rothman 1974). I handled this as long as I was aware of how I interrelated and interacted with the villagers. I asked them to tell me when I said or did something wrong. As long as they saw me react positively to their anecdotal observations by listening and practicing, they perceived that I really was interested in becoming a sensitive Yupiaq.

I have many relatives in the three villages. Some may have been a little jealous of my accomplishments, others may have had pet theories or projects that they would want me to support; both attitudes created problems for me at times. Depending on the situation, I most often would be merely a sounding board, the sympathetic listener. Morris Freilich calls this role "therapy capital" (1970). I did not want to get so politically and socially involved, however, that I had no time to do my own work.

Another problem area was moral conflict and value clashes. In order to compensate for this, I would listen to people talk, observe respected leaders' deportment, and, especially, the ways in which villagers conduct themselves during various meetings and gatherings (Pelto & Pelto 1970). Villagers, assuming that I knew more than I did about Yupiaq language and culture, made statements or did things without explaining themselves (Eisener

1991). When I did not understand the meaning of the word used or action, I asked for clarification. The meaning of the word may have changed over time. How did I develop a routine of attentiveness? J. Wilson states that "through his reason man observes himself, but only through consciousness does he know himself" (1969:150). I asked myself constantly, "Am I doing the right thing?" and "Am I doing OK?"

Another difficulty I had to overcome was seeing human misery. The Alaskan villages do not escape poverty. Children might be ill clothed or ill fed—long-existing problems. However, parents suffering from drug abuse or malaise of the spirit are frequently ineffectual as providers and homemakers. However, this adversity sometimes provided incentive and motivation for them to work for a greater degree of self-determination and self-reliance. In the past, the Yupiaq lived a life that required a balance between quality of life and an environmentally determined set of needs. If we could develop a new consciousness with a new Yupiaq identity and a cultural mix of chosen values, traditions, and customs, we would go a long way toward alleviating the physical and psychosocial problems we face and toward helping us find our place in the world (Gamble 1986). For too long, we have left the study of our values, habits, customs, beliefs, and ourselves as a people to outsiders, and likewise, the "solutions" to our problems have come from outside, often without consideration of our Yupiaq values and other human factors (Gamble 1986; Hau'ofa 1982).

One tenet of faith in Western science has been the so-called objectivity, but how can we truly be objective if we manipulate information in our minds? One cannot represent others except on one's own terms (Van Maanen 1988). This attempt at isolation restricts seeing or understanding as it applies to the real world (Gamble 1986; Nollman 1990). B. L. Whorf has said that "all observers are not led by the same physical evidence to the same picture of the universe, unless their linguistic backgrounds are similar or can in some way be calibrated" (cited in Gamble 1986).

I have cultural and educational biases which I took into the village, so I had to find a way to deal with the subjective and lessen its effect on me as a researcher. If I had let my feelings and emotions run rampant, I would have come out with a product slanted only to my prior way of thinking. It would have been an individual product. As a participant observer using the methods of listening, observing, interviewing, and interpreting visual arts, I think it important that I overcame a lot of potential subjectivity through discussion, ironing out differences of opinion, and maintaining a constant verbal and written exchange between myself and the villagers (Koetjaraningrat 1982). I had to learn routines of rigorous note taking, attempting accurate descriptions of observations and verbatim quotations of villagers (Gamble 1986; Pelto 1965). I had to learn what constitutes an effective appraisal of activities, conversations, and settings as being of value to our project (Van Maanen 1988). I had to practice writing accurate descriptions, especially at the beginning, for review by myself and others to see what observational biases might manifest themselves for me to correct in the future (Pelto 1965). This lent itself to coherence, insight, and the instrumental utility of seeing things in a way that satisfies, or is useful to me and to the villagers, leading to a gut feeling that it seems right (Eisener 1991).

Rigorous note taking required that I write down my impressions, hunches, and hard information during or soon after the event (Freilich 1970). It was helpful to write down summaries of what I thought I knew and what I know now (Freilich 1970). This began to show what biases I came with.

When a certain amount of information was gathered, I cross-checked the information for accuracy with villagers (Pelto 1965) and structured the information into cultural domains and themes for exploration of relationships (Pelto & Pelto 1970; Spradley 1979). Again, verbal or written summaries of the results were done for reactions by valued informants.

This form of community-based research was a mutual learning experience. The villagers and I experienced the reciprocal learning process involved in data gathering. My intellectual curiosity was piqued, and I learned to understand the decision-making processes, to hone interpersonal skills, and to (re)learn cooperative skills as a participant (Schug & Beery 1984). Community-based research looks at past ways of knowledge production and doing things as well as those of the present. We put into practice the notion that the human being "has the capacity to adopt, adapt, and reconstitute present and past ideas, beliefs and inventions of others who are living or dead" to make a new Yupiaq consciousness (Pelto 1965:102).

Domains and Instrumentation

This dissertation project was not intended to determine whether the Yupiaq people should return to a traditional way of life (if this were even possible), or try to expunge the modern from their life. Rather it is to delineate the choices that will need to be made in order to establish a quality of life that has a balance between their human needs and wants and what is available locally and naturally. Collaborative and integrative processes need to be undertaken. According to Robert E. Stake and Jack Easley, science can be conceptualized as inquiry, as explanation, or as science and technology (1978). Stephen Gould goes on to point out that "science must be understood as a social phenomenon, a gutsy, human enterprise, not the work of robots programmed to collect pure information" (1981:21).

For the Yupiaq, knowledge and skills are derived from their human effort to develop a worldview consonant with themselves, nature, and the spiritual world, so the Yupiaq youngster develops a sense of being part of the universe as a result of his or her culture's teaching and learning. The Yupiaq junior and senior high-school students enter school with a great deal of traditional scientific knowledge, most of which is ignored or not considered applicable to science teaching in the school, where science most often comes from textbooks, manuals, and teacher-directed learning activities. My observations and questioning of Yupiaq scientific knowledge and skills had a natural orientation; that is, I recorded observations and conversations as they occurred in a natural environment. The question then becomes whether the knowledge and skills that I observed in the community are reconcilable with the molecularization and sequencing approach used in the school. In the school, a definition of behavior to be taught, identification of components, and the sequential ordering for teaching purposes can be readily observed. The scientific method works well in the age-tested recipes for experiments in the classroom or laboratory, but how well does it work for transmitting the practical scientific knowledge used in the Yupiaq fish camp? How is traditional Yupiaq knowledge learned, and how is it understood by practitioners today? These are the kinds of questions to which my inquiry was directed.

Following is a list of some of the domains of activity in which I focused my initial observations, along with the kinds of instrumentation and documentation that I used to obtain data associated with each domain.

The findings from data gathering, along with other domains of analysis and sources of information, were cross-checked to determine the degree of representation and accuracy in the community.

Field Methodologies in Retrospect

Some of the methodological problems I tried to anticipate in preparation for the fieldwork were borne out and others were not. However, there were important issues that I did not foresee that became problematic, at least to me. My idea of being a participant-observer certainly did work out, but some of the tools that are spelled out by numerous authors did not work as I had anticipated. Although I had prepared sample questions for use in interviews (see Appendix 1), I had a difficult time doing the interviews with local people, especially the elders. There may have been some questioning methods or protocol that I did not follow. Whether they mistrusted me or wondered what I was going to do with the information they might share with me was not clear. But I was not fully satisfied with my planned interviews with elders.

The interviews with teachers worked out well. Of the nine teachers, one was an Alaska Native. They all willingly let me interview them, and I appreciated this very much. They opened their classrooms to me. The principal was very welcoming and very supportive of my project. He was the one who put the teachers at ease and let them know that I would be visiting their classrooms. The Tribal Council and Board of Education were very supportive and let it be known that I would be around, what I was trying to do, and that they were fully behind my efforts.

For men and women in the community, it became expedient and worked well that I informally visited with them wherever they happened to be—at the post office, the laundry, sitting on a log on the riverbank, chatting with women cutting fish, attending community activities at the school building, visiting at tribal or corporate offices, going drift netting with villagers, chatting at the village store, riding on a vehicle with elders, being invited to homes, and mostly just hanging around and observing people doing what they normally do. All this was done without a video camera or cassette recorder, and most often without a pencil and paper. Information and feelings were freely expressed, but it meant that I would have to listen very carefully and write down information and ideas as soon I got back to my room. I got pretty good at this after a while.

Other times I would take a camera, a pencil and paper, and just stroll through the village taking note of children at play, activities of grown-ups, or local adaptations of tools and machinery to fit their needs. I looked at design, construction, and use of old log homes, old frame houses, and new houses funded through the federal and state governments. I looked at the problems and kinds of pollution, and at the accumulation of trash outside the houses and around the village because the modern waste is no longer biodegradable.

The KYUK radio broadcasts from the nearby community of Bethel were an excellent source of information, especially their interviews and the storytelling by elders. It got so that I looked forward to the special times allotted to this very important activity. I jotted down notes and the names of people who participated. The elders often talked of values that were handed down through the ages, with the occasional diagnoses of the bases for current Yupiaq confusion, its causes and effects. The speakers included elders from the villages in the local area. All these added to the things that I had learned from my grandmother, family, community, and readings.

I had not anticipated deaths of close relatives, but it happened within three weeks of my arrival in the region. I was called upon to care for an uncle who was dying. It was a time of sadness and distress, and perhaps I did not perform my research very well during that time. I remember the very last time I saw him. I flew with him on an emergency flight to Bethel and was with him as he was admitted to the hospital. Now and then he would ask the doctor or nurse if I was still there in the emergency room. This was a responsibility I could not ignore. The other unanticipated experience was with my aunt, who never let on that she was terminally ill. She and her daughter had just returned from a visit to the Alaska Native Medical Center in Anchorage. She was happy to meet my youngest daughter for the first time. She fed us and talked and was very caring. She seemed to be very happy to be visiting, and I never expected to learn, only a short time later, that she had passed away a week after our visit with her. Both of these deaths affected my ability to focus on my fieldwork, but both were also instrumental in socializing me back into the way of life I was studying.

My observations and research may not always have adhered to the methods and techniques espoused by experienced field researchers. However, I believe that I had an advantage over most researchers attempting to address the issues of this study, in that I am a Yupiaq, I speak the language, I am very familiar with the Yupiaq sense of the sacred, and I experienced many changes in my own lifestyle while I was an exile and emigrant from my people for two decades after graduation from college. In retrospect, I see that I relied heavily on the traditional Yupiaq method of research—that is, patient observation through participation over a long period of time, reflection on things that I saw and heard, and, unobtrusively, informally checking out my tentative conclusions with villagers. I hope the results show that a tactful, adaptive approach to fieldwork produced the insights and information I was seeking.

Glossary

Akutaq A dessert made of oil, berries, and sugar.

Alerquutet Instructions to live by.

Angiatuli To unravel the chaos of weather permutations to make predictions.

Anlleq Mouse food gathered from the roots of a reed.

Carangllut All plants.

Cukneq To measure.

Cuqtaariyaraq The process of measuring.

Ella Depending on usage in the sentence, this word could mean weather, outside, sky, earth, universe, or consciousness.

Ella amigligtuq The sky is cloudy.

Ellagpiim yua Spirit of the universe.

Ellam nunii The world's land.

Ellam yua Spirit of the universe, equivalent to God, or the Great Mystery.

Ellapak Universe.

Iinruk An object possessing mystical power.

Inerquutet Warnings to avoid becoming a worldly person.

Mamterilleq A village (Bethel) whose name means "a place of many smokehouses."

Mell'gag A curved carving knife.

Nunalikut The village is saddened, for example, by death of a community member.

Nunam gainga mamkillrani When the world's crust was thin.

Piciyarat The ways to be.

Qaill' ella auqa How is the weather?

Qaill' ellan auqa How are you feeling?

Qaluyaat Nelson Island.

Qaneryaraat Proverbs or oral teachings.

Qanganaruat Name for wormwood, often used for medicinal purposes.

Qasegiq Men's community house.

Qayaq Skin-covered watercraft having a single hole for the user.

Quyana Thank you.

Tangruak Pretend to see.

Tangruarluki kanginguakluki To visualize to understand a phenomenon.

Tangruarluki To see with the mind's eye; visualize.

Tepa Fish buried underground and allowed to ferment; called stink heads.

Tuaii, am'llegiuk Finished, it has gotten to be much.

Tununermiut Dwellers of the village of Tununak.

Uluaq Woman's cutting knife.

Una taringeqerciu Understand this.

Wagaa Hello.

Waten Like this.

Waten piliku Do it this way.

Yungnaqsarat Rules for making a life.

Yupiaq Original term for a "real person"; it is the same as the modern term Yup'ik.

Bibliography

Alexie, O., and H. Morris. 1985. *The Elders' Conference, 1984*. Bethel, AK: Orutsararmiut Native Council.

Altorki, S. 1982. "The Anthropologist in the Field: A Case of Indigenous Anthropology from Saudi Arabia." In H. Fahim, ed., *Indigenous Anthropology in Non-Western Countries*. Durham: Carolina Academic Press.

American Indian Lawyer Training Program. 1988. *Indian Tribes as Sovereign Governments*. Oakland, CA: American Indian Lawyer Training Center.

Anderson, J. M. 1991. *Northern Science for Northern Society: Building Economic Self-Reliance*. Ottawa: Science Council of Canada.

Augros, R., and G. Stanciu. 1987. *The New Biology*. Boston: New Science Library.

Bakar, O. B. 1991. "The Unity of Science and Spiritual Knowledge." In R. Ravindra, ed., *Science and Spirit*. New York: Paragon House.

Barnes, J. A. 1982. "Social Science in India: Colonial Import, Indigenous Product, or Universal Truth?" In H. Fahim, ed., *Indigenous Anthropology in Non-Western Countries*. Durham: Carolina Academic Press.

Barnhardt, R. 1977. "Administrative Influences in Alaskan Native Education." In R. Barnhardt, ed., *Cross-cultural Issues in Alaskan Education*. Fairbanks, AK: Center for Northern Educational Research.

Berger, P. L. 1976. *Pyramids of Sacrifice*. New York: Anchor Doubleday.

Berger, P., B. Berger, and H. Kellner. 1974. *The Homeless Mind: Modernization and Consciousness*. New York: Vintage Books.

Bielawski, E. 1990. *Cross-cultural Epistemology: Cultural Readaptation Through the Pursuit of Knowledge*. Paper presented at the 7th Inuit Studies Conference. Fairbanks: University of Alaska-Fairbanks.

Blatchford, E. 1990. "AFN Praises Passage of Native Policy Commission Legislation." *The Tundra Drums*, p. 13. Aug. 16, 1990 Bethel, AK.

Bodley, J. H. 1982. *Victims of Progress*. Menlo Park, CA: Benjamin/ Cummings.

Briggs, J. 1992. *Fractals: The Patterns of Chaos*. New York: Simon & Schuster.

Burger, J. 1990. *First Peoples*. New York: Anchor Doubleday.

Caduto, M. J., and J. Bruchac. 1989. *Keepers of the Earth*. Saskatoon: Fifth House Publishers.

Cajete, G. A. 1986. *Science: A Native American Perspective*. Unpublished.

Capra, F. 1984. *The Tao of Physics*. New York: Bantam.

Chrisjohn, R., S. Towson, and M. Peters. 1988. "Indian Achievement in School: Adaptation to Hostile Environments." In J. W. Berry, S. H. Irvine, and E. B. Hunt, eds., *Indigenous Cognition: Functioning in Cultural Context*. Boston: Marinus Nijhoff.

Cohen, Y. A. 1982. "Studying a Nation-State Anthropologically." In H. Fahim, ed., *Indigenous Anthropology in Non-Western Countries*. Durham: Carolina Academic Press.

Cole, K. C. 1986. *Things Your Teacher Never Told You About Science*. Boulder, CO: American Indian Science and Engineering Society.

Collier, J. 1973. *Alaskan Eskimo Education: A Film Analysis of Cultural Confrontation in the Schools*. New York: Holt, Rinehart and Winston.

Collier, M. 1979. *A Film Study of Classrooms in Western Alaska*. Fairbanks: Center for Cross-cultural Studies, University of Alaska-Fairbanks.

Cornell, E. A. 1986. *Preparing Teachers to Teach Science*. Boulder, CO: American Indian Science and Engineering Society.

Darnell, F. 1979. "Education Among the Native Peoples of Alaska." *Polar Record* 19:431–446.

Darwin, C. 1859. *The Origin of Species*. London: J. Murray.

Deloria, V., Jr. 1990. "Traditional Technology." *Winds of Change* 5:12–17.

Deloria, V., Jr. 1991a. "Higher Education and Self-Determination." *Winds of Change* 6:18–25.

Deloria, V., Jr. 1991b. "The Perpetual Education Report." *Winds of Change* 6:12–18.

Egede, I. 1985. "Educational Problems in Greenland." *Arctic Medical Research* 40:32–36.

Eisner, E. 1991. *The Enlightened Eye*. New York: Macmillan.

Fahim, H., ed., 1982. *Indigenous Anthropology in Non-Western Countries*. Durham: Carolina Academic Press.

Fienup-Riordan, A. 1990. *Eskimo Essays: Yup'ik Lives and How We See Them*. New Brunswick, NJ: Rutgers University Press.

Fienup-Riordan, A. 1991. *The Real People and the Children of Thunder: The Yup'ik Eskimo Encounter with Moravian Missionaries John and Edith Kilbuck*. Norman: University of Oklahoma Press.

Flanders, N. E. 1988. *Natives and Knowledge Studies of the Inupiat, Public Policy, and Anthropological Knowledge*. Hanover, NH: Dartmouth College.

Forbes, N. 1984. *The Impact of Television in Rural Alaska*. Fairbanks: Center for Cross-cultural Studies, University of Alaska-Fairbanks.

Fortuine, R. 1989. *Chills and Fever*. Fairbanks: University of Alaska Press.

Franklin, U. 1990. *The Real World of Technology*. Toronto: CBC Enterprises.

Freeman, M., M. R. Milton, and Ludwig N. Carbyn. 1988. *Traditional Knowledge and Renewable Resource Management in Northern Regions*. Edmonton: IUCN Commission on Ecology and the Boreal Institute for Northern Studies.

Freilich, M. 1970. *Marginal Natives: Anthropologists at Work*. New York: Harper and Row.

Gamble, D. J. 1986. "Crushing of Cultures: Western Applied Science in Northern Societies." *Arctic* 39:20–23.

Geertz, C. 1973. *The Interpretation of Cultures*. New York: Basic Books.

Gould, S. J. 1981. *The Mismeasure of Man*. New York: W. W. Norton.

Greer, S. 1992. "Building from Ancient Values: The Harmonic Visions of Architect Douglas J. Cardinal." *Winds of Change* 7:198–205.

Guyette, S. 1983. *Community-based Research: A Handbook for Native Americans*. Los Angeles: American Indian Studies Center.

Halifax, J. 1979. *Shamanic Voices: A Survey of Visionary Narratives*. New York: E. P. Dutton.

Hall, S. 1988. *The Fourth World: The Heritage of the Arctic and Its Destruction*. New York: Vintage Books.

Harding, S. and M. Hintikka. 1983. *Discovering Reality: Feminist Perspectives on Epistemology, Metaphysics, Methodology, and Philosophy of Science*. Boston: D. Reidel.

Hardwick, S. 1991. "I Serve Them . . . I Am Their Leader." *Winds of Change* 6:32–37.

Harrison, P. 1983. *The Third World Tomorrow*. Markham, Ontario: Pilgrim Press.

Hau'ofa, E. 1982. "Anthropology at Home: A South Pacific Islands Experience." In H. Fahim, ed., *Indigenous Anthropology in Non-Western Countries*. Durham: Carolina Academic Press.

Henkelman, J. W., and K. H. Vitt. 1985. *Harmonious to Dwell*. Bethel, AK: Tundra Press.

Hensley, W. L. 1989. *Helping Schools Succeed at Helping All Children Learn*. Juneau, AK: 15th Alaska Legislature.

Hobson, G. 1992. "Traditional Knowledge Is Science." *Northern Perspectives* 20:2.

Hopkins, D. M., W. H. Arundale, and C. W. Slaughter. 1990. *Science in Northwest Alaska: Research Needs and Opportunities on Federally Protected Lands*. Fairbanks: Alaska Quaternary Center, University of Alaska-Fairbanks.

Hopson, E. 1977. "Inupiaq Education." In R. Barnhardt, ed., *Cross-cultural Issues in Alaskan Education*. Fairbanks: Center for Northern Educational Research, University of Alaska-Fairbanks.

Kaplan, L. D., ed., 1988. *Ugiuvangmiut Quliapyuit*. Fairbanks: University of Alaska Press.

Kashoki, M. E. 1982. "Indigenous Scholarship in African Universities: The Human Factor." In H. Fahim, ed., *Indigenous Anthropology in Non-Western Countries*. Durham: Carolina Academic Press.

Kawagley, O. 1990. "Yup'ik Ways of Knowing." *Canadian Journal of Native Education* 17:5–17.

Kirkness, V. J. 1977. *Tanzania's Policy Directive "Education for Self-Reliance" and National Indian Brotherhood's Policy Paper "Indian Control of Indian Education*. Vancouver: First Nations House of Learning, University of British Columbia.

Knudtson, P., and D. Suzuki. 1992. *Wisdom of the Elders*. Toronto: Stoddart.

Koetjaraningrat. 1982. "Anthropology in Developing Countries." In H. Fahim, ed., *Indigenous Anthropology in Non-Western Countries*. Durham: Carolina Academic Press.

Lindblom, C. E., and D. K. Cohen. 1979. *Usable Knowledge*. New Haven: Yale University Press.

Livingston, J. A. 1981. *The Fallacy of Wildlife Conservation*. Toronto: McClelland and Stewart.

Locust, C. 1988. "Wounding the Spirit: Discrimination and Traditional American Indian Belief Systems." *Harvard Educational Review* 58:315–331.

Lopez, B. 1986. *Arctic Dreams: Imagination and Desire in a Northern Landscape*. New York: Bantam Books.

Lovelock, J. E. 1987. *Gaia*. New York: Oxford University Press.

Lovins, A. B. 1977. *Soft Energy Paths*. New York: Harper & Row.

Madan, T. N. 1982. "Indigenous Anthropology in Non-Western Countries: An Overview." In H. Fahim, ed., *Indigenous Anthropology in Non-Western Countries*. Durham: Carolina Academic Press.

Madsen, E. 1983. *The Akiak "Contract School": A Case Study of Revitalization in an Alaskan Village*. Ph.D. diss., University of Oregon.

Martin, B. 1991. "Storytelling and Five Women Leaders." *Winds of Change* 6:23–28.

Milbrath, L. W. 1989. *Envisioning a Sustainable Society*. Albany: State University of New York Press.

Mills, S. 1990. *In Praise of Nature*. Covelo, CA: Island Press.

Momaday, N. S. 1969. *The Way to Rainy Mountain*. Albuquerque: University of New Mexico Press.

Morris, D. 1969. *The Human Zoo*. New York: Dell.

Muktoyuk, M. 1988. *Inupiaq Rules for Living*. Anchorage: AMU Press.

Murchie, S. 1981. *Seven Mysteries of the Universe*. New York: Knopf.

Nakane, C. 1982. "The Effect of Cultural Tradition on Anthropologists." In H. Fahim, ed., *Indigenous Anthropology in Non-Western Countries*. Durham: Carolina Academic Press.

Napoleon, H. 1991. Yuuyaraq: *The Way of the Human Being*. Fairbanks: Center for Cross-cultural Studies, University of Alaska-Fairbanks.

Nelson, R. K. 1983. *Make Prayers to the Raven*. Chicago: University of Chicago Press.

Netting, R. M. 1986. *Cultural Ecology*. Prospect Heights, IL: Waveland Press.

Nollman, J. 1990. *Spiritual Ecology: A Guide to Reconnecting with Nature*. New York: Bantam.

Nyerere, J. K. 1968. *Ujamaa: Essays on Socialism*. London: Oxford University Press.

Okoko, K. A. B. 1987. *Socialism and Self-reliance in Tanzania*. New York: Harcourt.

Omari, I. M. 1990. *Innovation and Change in Higher Education in Developing Countries: Experiences from Tanzania*. Vancouver: Center for Policy Studies, University of British Columbia.

Oswalt, W. 1963. *Mission of Change in Alaska: Eskimos and Moravians on the Kuskokwim*. San Marino, CA: Huntington Library.

Oswalt, W. H. 1990. *Bashful No Longer*. Norman: University of Oklahoma Press.

Page, M. 1989. *The Tao of Power*. London: Green Print.

Pelto, P. 1965. *The Study of Anthropology*. Columbus, OH: Charles E. Merrill.

Pelto, P., and G. H. Pelto. 1978. *Anthropological Research: The Structure of Inquiry*. Cambridge: Cambridge University Press.

Petersen, R. 1982. "Some Ethical Questions in Connection with Research Activity in an Asymmetrical Ethnic Situation." In H. Fahim, ed., *Indigenous Anthropology in Non-Western Countries*. Durham: Carolina Academic Press.

Pickering, A. 1992. *Science as Practice and Culture*. Chicago: University of Chicago Press.

Piniaqtavut Committee 1989. *Piniaqtavut Integrated Program*. Iqaluit, N.W.T.: Baffin Divisional Board of Education.

Pratt, C. 1976. *The Critical Phase in Tanzania, 1945–1968*. Cambridge: Cambridge University Press.

Ravindra, R. 1991. *Science and Spirit*. New York: Paragon House.

Rifkin, J. 1980. *Entropy*. New York: Viking.

Roads, M. J. 1985. *Talking with Nature*. Tiburon: H. J. Dramer.

Rothman, J. 1974. *Planning and Organizing for Social Change*. New York: Columbia University Press.

Ryan, J. 1989. "Disciplining the Innut: Normalization, Characterization, and Schooling." *Curriculum Inquiry* 19:379–403.

Sahlins, M. 1972. *Stone Age Economics*. Chicago: Aldine Atherton.

Schug, M. C., and R. Beery. 1984. *Community Study: Applications and Opportunities*. Washington, DC: National Council for the Social Studies.

Schumacher, E. F. 1977. *A Guide for the Perplexed*. New York: Harper & Row.

Schwalbe, A. B. 1951. *Dayspring on the Kuskokwim*. Bethlehem, PA: Moravian Church.

Scollon, R., and S. Scollon. 1979. "Bush Consciousness and Modernization." In R. Scollon and S. Scollon, *Linguistic Convergence: An Ethnography of Speaking at Fort Chipewyan, Alberta*. New York: Academic Press.

Sivertsen, M. 1990. *Science Education Programs That Work*. Washington, DC: Office of Educational Research and Improvement, U.S. Department of Education.

Simonelli, R. 1991. "Caucasian Tears: An Engineer Reflects on Technology and Traditional Ways." *Winds of Change* 6:52–61.

Spradley, J. P. 1979. *The Ethnographic Interview*. New York: Holt, Rinehart and Winston.

Spradley, J. P. 1980. *Participant Observation*. New York: Holt, Rinehart and Winston.

Stake, R., and J. A. J. Easley. 1978. *Case Studies in Science Education*. Washington, DC: National Science Foundation.

Vanderwerth, W. C. 1971. *Indian Oratory*. New York: Ballantine.

Van Maanen, J. 1988. *Tales of the Field*. Chicago: University of Chicago Press.

Van Manen, M. 1990. *Researching Lived Experience*. Ann Arbor, MI: Edwards Brothers.

Weaver, H. 1988. "A People in Peril." *Anchorage Daily News*.

Wilson, J. 1969. *Thinking with Concepts*. Cambridge: Cambridge University Press.

Yupitak, Bista. 1977. "Does One Way of Life Have to Die so that Another Can Live?" Bethel: A Report on Subsistence and the Conservation of the Yupik Life-style.